VEGETARIAN
OR
NON-VEGETARIAN

CHOOSE YOURSELF

by

Gopi Nath Aggarwal

BOOKS FOR ALL
[A Division of D. K. Publishers Distributors (P) Ltd.]
Delhi - 110052

Published with Permission From:
NABHI KUMAR JAIN
for Sanyam Baba Charitable Trust,
5041/3, Sant Nagar, Karol Bagh
New Delhi -110005

Published by:
BOOKS FOR ALL
[A Division of D.K. Publishers Distributors (P) Ltd.]
Regd Office: A-6, Nimri Community Centre,
Near Bharat Nagar, Ashok Vihar Phase IV, Delhi-110052

Printed by:
D.K.FINE ART PRESS
C-2/9, Community Centre
Ashok Vihar, Phase II,
Delhi-110052

Contents

1 *Why this Book?*

Ever since my childhood, I, Nabhi Kumar Jain, son of Shri Shanti Prashad Jain, had the privilege of learning the importance of religion, principles of life and death and the essence of the soul from my revered father. He enlightened my path and removed my doubts with arguments and apt illustrations. In my childhood I used to go for a morning walk with my father's elder brother Late Shri Jaini Mal Jain (M/s J.M. Jaina & Bros.) He daily used to feed crows, pigeons and sparrows; I observed how on seeing my uncle all those birds felt happy and flocked around him with cheer. The way my uncle fed the birds with care and affection, made me feel of the existence of some common bond of life and relation between man and his winged friends. No barriers of being human and birds or any communication gap stood between the love and affection of my uncle and his feathered companions.

The philosophy and deeds of my revered father and uncle impressed my searching mind so much that whenever I saw some one being tortured, I felt myself being tortured. My eternal mind used to rebel on seeing birds struggling in their cages. On releasing them from their confinement I got a feeling of having freed some one close to me. I always felt that all living beings are related to each other and have been their well wishers in any of their earlier births. So they were made to care for each other. This developed a philosophy in my psyche and now it is my firm conviction that if it ever came to a choice between consuming non vegetarian food or surrendering my own life, I would prefer the latter alternative.

I reduced use of leather goods even from my childhood and gradually discarded wearing leather footwear. During the days of my early professional life, I once asked my respected uncle Devendraji to apply for purchase of shares of a renowned Shoe Company. His response came as a beacon light for the path of my life. He said "Son, when God is otherwise so kind to me, why should I make leather as a source of my income?" These words had such an impact on me that I decided to renounce any source of income involving violence to any living creature directly or indirectly.

Earlier, our shop M/s JAIN BOOK AGENCY, New Delhi, used to stock books on subjects of rearing of poultry, fish and pigs besides other subjects. One day, on seeing these books in our shop, Dr. Kailash Chand Jain (of Raja Toys) remarked that we were participating in encouraging violence towards animals by stocking such books. From that day onwards, with the permission of my father and elder brother Shri Vimal Vahan Jain, who had the profoundest affection for me, I stopped stocking and selling books on rearing of poultry, fish and pigs. Sale of books containing recipes on all sorts of non vegetarian food was also stopped. By doing so, we had novel peace of mind and deepest satisfaction and by God's grace our business grew by leaps and bounds.

Three years ago, we purchased one thousand copies of the book *"Anda, Zahar Hi Zahar"* (Egg is only Poison) written by Dr. Nemi Chand Jain of Indore and displayed them on the counter of our shop (M/s Jain Book Agency) for free distribution. By the grace of God, people from all sections of the society belonging to various religions and from every corner of the country visit our shop. When some of the egg-eaters among them told me that after reading this book they had stopped consuming eggs, it gave me immense pleasure, and satisfaction. At the same time it occured to me that we should ourselves bring out a book on the respective merits and demerits of vegetarian and non vegetarian food. My aim was that this book should examine from scientific point of view the effects of food on health as also on mental and moral behaviour of human beings. Instead of imposing the decision about type of food best suited for human beings, idea was to give sufficient details about two types of food to help the readers to decide for themselves the most appropriate food for them.

As this idea dwelled on me, I requested my uncle (Mausajee) Shri Gopi Nath Aggarwal, D-12/3 Model Town, Delhi who is the author of *Shri Krishna Charit Manas, Chinta Mukti* & *Lok Vyavahar* etc. to write a book on this subject in tune with my sentiments and views. He gladly agreed to my request and the book he wrote is before you.

At the time of idea of bringing out this publication, I never imagined that within a span of few months, this book would become a crusade for vegetarianism. Taking inspiration from this book thousands of persons have already renounced flesh foods, whereas several others have devoted themselves to the hurculean task of conveying the message of this book to every home. Inspired by this book, the family members of M/s. D.K. Publishers and Distributors, Delhi. Shri Ishwar Chand Mittal and his sons, Shri Praveen, Pramod, Permil and Pradip Mittal have been offering their continued selfless cooperation in its printing, publicity and distribution. Their ideal will surely inspire many others to ofter similar cooperation in this crusade for vegetarianism.

Dear brothers and sisters, after reading this book and weighing in your mind the respective merits and demerits of vegetarian and non-vegetarian foods, decide for yourself which type of food is most appropriate and beneficial for your all round and overall development.

Praying for your good health and prosperity in life,

Nabhi Kumar Jain

2 Vegetarianism Vs. Non-vegetarianism

The scholars and saints of every religion of the world–Hindus, Muslims, Sikhs, Christians, Jains, Buddhists and others – have described violence, cruelty, untruth, anger and hatred as sins. Needless hurt and the infliction of pain on other living beings has been decried by all of them as equally sinful. Non-violence, kindness, forgiveness and truthfulness are described as *Dharma* or religion. Their main teaching is to see in every living being the image of the great Heavenly Father and to deal with them accordingly. They not only condemned eating of flesh for food but also taught mankind to treat all living beings, animals, birds etc. with compassion and feed them with grains which was described as an act of kindness.

Nature has also provided innumerable tasty and nutritious vegetable products for human consumption while at the same time created various birds and animals to help and serve the mankind. These birds and animals not only lend a helping hand in maintaining the balance of nature, but on being accorded little bit of love and affection, serve the mankind from the core of their hearts and become more faithful and loyal than even their fellow human beings.

It is definitely an act of total misconduct and ungrr tefulness that man whose body has been made by nature akin to the body structure of vegetarian species and different from that of meat-eating species, goes against nature and defies the teachings of saints and sages and consumes meat. All living beings – like us – are creations of the same Almighty. Will the Heavenly father tolerate the crime of killing his children by his other progeny without any justification? No, never! One will always be paid in the same kind for his deeds. No action either good or bad ever goes unrewarded. Sooner or later, we are sure to be rewarded or punished for our deeds. This is an unalterable, inevitable and universal truth.

Today, doctors and scientists from every corner of the world are warning that flesh-foods induce cancer and incurable diseases and shorten the life-span, whereas vegetarian foods yield more nutrition and enhance the body's immunity to fight diseases, promoting health and long life. Most of the animals used for food eat sorts of unhygenic eatables and are likely to have harmful infection in their body. Imagine the plight of person who consumes such flesh and becomes prone to innumerable diseases. If even then, human beings continue to destroy themselves by eating flesh-food, either in blind race of copying others or in the pursuit of so called modernity, it can only be called their misfortune or ill luck.

Before slaughtering animals for food, no adequate examination is made of the diseases they harbour in their bodies and thus their diseases enter the bodies of those who consume their flesh. Besides this, the cruel and torturous atmosphere in which these animals are killed, creates a lot of fear, tension and anger which further makes the meat poisonous. This poisonous and disease – infested meat, on consumption, induces lots of incurable diseases and it seems that it fulfils the killed animal's curse, "As you consume me, so will I consume you."

Oh, my non-vegetarian brethren, before you get ready to eat meat the next time, please do pay a visit to the poultry farm and slaughter house to see with your own eyes the torture inflicted on these silent victims, their pain and suffering and the ghastly expressions on the faces of these animals. Then ask your conscience whether our superiority and humanity lie only in the selfish perception of our taste-buds and in snatching for ever life out of these living beings which we can never give back.

Dear brothers, please look into the pros and cons of your own interest. Flesh-foods instead of providing nutrition, give you incurable diseases and diminish your life-span. Such foods pollute your minds and hearts, destroy your happiness and peace of mind, leading to decline of morals and character, pushing not only yourselves but also your coming generations towards incurable diseases and unsurmountable troubles. For the sake of saving your children whom you love more than your own lives, from the dangers of cancer, heart ailments and other social disadvantages, please stop consumption of flesh-foods right from today itself. Every moment is the right moment for repentence. According to the scriptures, "Those who renounce flesh-foods are equally rewarded as those who perform a *yajna*".

3 *What should be a Man's Food?*

Next to air and water the most important requisite for a human being to stay alive is food. What should one eat? What is the objective of food? How much should one eat? These are the questions which need due consideration.

What is the objective of food? The object of man's food is not just to fill his belly, to maintain health or to satisfy his taste but to properly develop his mind and character too. Our intake of food is closely related with our thinking, character and deeds. Age old saying "The kind of food you eat determines the kind of man you are", is equally applicable today also. The taste of a man in different types of food reflects his behaviour and character. In fact it is an indicator of one's innermost self. Hence, the objective of our diet should be to consume only those items which contribute to our physical, moral, social and spiritual uplift and promote love, affection, compassion, non violence, peace and similar values of life.

What type of food we need? Our food should contain all those ingredients which produce energy, health and heat. Our food should have proteins, sugar, vitamins, minerals and fats in adequate quantities and right proportion so that good quality of new cells and R.B.Cs (Red Blood Corpuscles) are produced *continuously. Because in our system, millions of R.B.Cs are produced and destroyed every second. It is estimated that in each duration of six years, all the cells and tissues of our body are completely replaced. As the snake changes its old skin by the new one every six months, similarly our body also changes its all cells and tissues every sixth year, and the quality of these new cells depends on the quality of our intake of food.

---

* Ahinsa voice, Jan. 90 published by Sharman Sahitya Sansthan, Delhi.

Simultaneously, our food should contain substances which help build up our body's defence system or immunity from disease and do not interfere in expulsion of waste materials and toxins. Our food should not contain substances which are disease inducing, which destroy health and which create excitement and affect us emotionally, phychologically and create imbalance and lack of self control and discipline in the body.

Food requirement of our body : Nature has created for us so many kind of foodgrains, fruits, nuts, leaves and vegetables etc. which contain all types of nutritional ingredients in sufficient quantity. One's daily requirement of different ingredients is given on next page.

* Person	Protein gms.	Fat gms.	Calories
Man (Moderate Work)	60	15	2700
Man (Sedentary Work)	60	15	2350
Woman (Moderate Work)	50	15	2100
Woman (Sedentary Work)	50	15	1800
Boy (13-15 yrs.)	71	15	2400
Girl (13-15 yrs.)	67	15	2050

The above requirements can be adequately obtained from the following vegetarian foods.

* Item	Quantity Grams	Protein	Fat	Calories
Cereals	400	48.4	6.8	1384
Pulses	60	14.6	7.3	209
Leafy Green Vegetables	100	2.0	0.7	26
Other Vegetables	75	2.0	0.3	22
Roots & Tubers	75	1.2	–	72
Fruits	50	0.3		24
Milk	250	8.0	10.2	168
Fats	25		25.0	225
Sugar	30			120
Total		76.5	50.3	2250

* Nutritive value of Indian Foods, issued by National Institute of Nutrition, ICMR, Hyderabad.

According to your taste and financial status you can prepare both cheap and costly, balanced and nutritional vegetarian diet by selecting various items from the list of products given on Page 11. Vegetarian foods not only cost less but also increases the resistance power of our body against diseases, thereby saving our health, money and time. Raw and uncooked vegetables and fruits are well known for their qualities in curing many ailments. Certain type of dietry fibres which are found in plant foods only, help to keep the blood cholesterol level low and offer protection against diabetes and many other diseases.

How much to eat? Many more people die of over-eating than of starvation. Eating a bit less is much better than to eat more. We must remember that "We eat to live and not live to eat". Thus our food intake should be slightly less than our hunger as like many other bodily functions, eating also is a matter of habit. People doing same kind of work and of same age group, do not eat equal quantity of food. Some eat more while some eat less. Those who eat less are by no means less healthy than those who eat more. Nor are those who eat costly stuff stronger than those who eat cheaper nutritional food. Those who eat more than their appetite, become victims of obesity which tends to make them lazy and sluggish, leading to indigestion, constipation and other ailments. Over-eating is the main and root cause of most diseases.

There is a saying "Bigger the waistline shorter is life line". The great Sufi saint Sheikh Saadi, advised that only half of one's stomach should be filled by food, one quarter should be filled with water, the remaining quarter should be left empty and that would be filled with the glory of God. Eating more due to tasty foods invite problems for one's health. Shastras have advised both the students as well as Saadhaks (spiritual practitioners) to eat sparingly and described it as an essential pre-requisite for the success of their endeavours.

One of the biggest advantage of the vegetarian food is

that it is bulky and satisfies our hunger quickly. It contains less cholasterol and is usually less spicy. As such it is difficult to eat more vegetarian food than the requirement of the body. The obestity thus remains under check.

Our body is a wonderfully complex machine which is constantly engaged in many activities like breathing in and out, purifying and circulating the blood, producing fresh blood, digesting, expelling toxins and waste products from the system and numerous other functions. Like other machines, this machine also requires some rest, which we can give it by observing fast once a week. This practice will reduce pressure on our digestive system and on the kidneys, and avoid many kinds of diseases. More food does not mean more health. The less you pour into this machine the more efficiently will it work for you, and the more you give it, the less productive it will be for you. "Food is made for us and we are not made for food", hence to remain healthy our principle should be "Eat less – have more patience".

Difference between hunger of body and mind : In order to justify all his actions, man often says that he has to do everything to satisfy the hunger of his body. It is a fact that hunger of body makes every person restless and forces him to tread on a wrong path but it is much more true that the demand of hunger of body is very limited and he can fulfil it by little bit of hard work without resort to sinful or criminal actions. The hunger which never satisfies and for which one does so many wrong deeds, is not the hunger of body but is in fact the hunger of mind. This malaise of mind goes on increasing. The more one tries to satisfy it, the more it grows and leads him to cheating, fraud, arson, crime, murder and other bad habits resulting in fear, tension, anger and hatred, which are the main causes of all bad deeds and diseases.

It is often said that hunger of stomach has been satisfied but not of mind. This ever hungry mind creates most of the problems for us. As such it is in the interest of man to understand the difference between these two types of hungers.

4 Nature Made Human Body Like Vegetarian Animals

Numerous species of herbivores (vegetarian animals) as well as carnivores (flesh eating animals) inhabit in this universe. Some are very small while others have large sized bodies, but there is a marked difference in herbivorous and carnivores animals as far as their bodily structure, hands, feet, teeth, intestines, sense of seeing, smelling and style of eating, drinking etc. are concerned. For example –

1. Carnivores have sharp pointed teeth and claws with such nails as help them in tearing apart their prey easily.

Herbivores have teeth embedded in flat jaws. Their claws do not have sharp nails but are framed as such to pluck fruits etc. easily.

2. The iower jaws of carnivores move only upward and downward and they swallow their food without mastication.

The jaws of herbivores can move up and down, left and right i.e. in all directions. They swallow their food after chewing it.

3. The tongue of meat eating animals is very rough. They protrude it outwards to drink water.

The tongue of vegetarian animals is quite smooth. They use their lips rather than a protruding tongue to drink.

4. The length of intestines of carnivores is less, almost equal to the length of their bodies and about six times the length of their torso. Due to small intestines they throw out the flesh food before it gets contaminated and poisoned.

Herbivores have longer intestines, about four times their body-length or twelve times the torso, which cannot quickly expel any flesh-food.

5. The liver and kidney of meat eating animals are larger in proportion due to which they can throw out the waste material of meat easily.

The liver and kidney of vegetarian animals are smaller in proportion and unable to throw out the animal waste easily.

6. The hydrochloric acid content in the digestive system of carnivores is ten times more as compared to that of human beings which digests the meat easily. The hydrochloric acid content in vegetarian species is much less and so unable to digest meat easily.

7. The saliva of flesh eaters is acidic. The saliva of vegetarian species is alkaline and it contains Ptyaline which is helpful in digesting carbohydrates.

8. Carnivores have low Blood-PH, i.e., it tends to be acidic.

Herbivores have higher Blood-PH, i.e., it tends to be on alkaline side.

9. The Blood Lipo-Proteins of the carnivores are different from those of herbivores.

In human beings, the Blood-Lipo-Proteins are similar to those of the herbivores.

10. Carnivores have a very strong sense of smell, their eyes glow in the night and their night-vision is as good as in the day-time. These powers help them in killing their prey.

The sense of smell among herbivores is not so strongly developed and their night-vision is no where as good as day-vision.

11. The sound of meat eating animals is very coarse and frightening.

The sound of vegetarian animals is not coarse.

12. The visual power of kids of meat-eating animals is almost zero for about a week after their birth. The off-spring of vegetarian animals have normal sight, right from their birth.

The above facts go to prove that nature has made human body similar to those of vegetarian species like cow, horse, elephant, camel, giraffe and bulls etc. The various parts of human body are designed for obtaining and digesting only vegetable foods. Except for man, no other animal wants to behave in contravention of the bodily structure and faculties with which nature has endowed it. The lion will never eat grass even if it is hungry and a cow will never take flesh even if starving, because that is not their natural food and not compatible with their psyche and body structure. Meat eating animals spend their entire lives on flesh, for them it is a complete food. But no human being can survive for more than two three weeks alone on flesh-foods because a diet of meat alone will give rise to so much acidity and toxins inside his entrails as to upset the whole system. Even those persons who go against the laws of nature and consume meat, have to eat some vegetarian material also, because for man flesh is not a complete diet and it also reduces the life span. Eskimos, whose circumstances and environment compel them to subsist mostly on meat, have an average life span of only thirty years, whereas a man can live a long and healthy life on purely vegetarian diet.

*Dr. Allen Walker of Johns Hopkins University has found by microscopic analysis of teeth that man is a descendent of fruit eating animals and not of carnivores.

No human being feels disgusted at the sight or smell of fruits, vegetables or cereals, while most people feel hatred by the sight of slaughtered animals hanging in butcher's shop. Is it not an obvious pointer to their vegetarian nature?

All the above mentioned facts prove that nature has designed man to be a vegetarian and only vegetarian. Feeding of non-vegetarian food for which the system is not designed can cause only harm and weaken the God gifted body.

---

* Jane Brody's Nutrition Book Nov. 1981.

5 Vegetarian Diet : More Nutritious & Beneficial

In blind pursuit of so-called modernity, people who describe their own culture, thinking and traditions as primitive and outdated are falling prey to the false assumption that vegetarian food does not provide adequate proteins and nutrition for body building. This is pure delusion. Modern researchers and scientists have found clear evidence that vegetarian food not only provides high quality proteins but also supplies all the other necessary nutritive elements like vitamins and minerals of high calorific value. Soyabeans and ground nuts contain more proteins than meat and eggs. Protein content is no less even in common pulses. If green vegetables and pulses are taken in adequate quantity with wheat, rice, jawar, bajra, and maize etc. they not only meet the requirement of proteins but also provide a more balanced nutritive diet, which makes the vegetarian healthier, stronger and long living than the non-vegetarian. Again, meat has no taste of its own. The spices, fats etc. which are added in its cooking lend it their flavour and taste. Whereas all the vegetarian food items like fruit, vegetable, root nut or tuber etc. have a distinct taste of their own and can be eaten without adding anything.

Looking at the animal world, we find that most powerful, hard-working and tolerant animals who can work continuously for days at a stretch like elephant, horse, bull and camel etc. are all pure vegetarians. Recent researches in England have revealed that when hunting dogs which are meat eaters by nature were kept on a vegetarian diet, they exhibited greater tolerance and enhanced endurance and ability.

Tensing Sherpa, the conqueror of Mount Everest, has disclosed that the secret behind the energy and strength of the

Sherpas is that they are vegetarians. Many international players and athletes are also renouncing flesh foods now and turning to vegetarianism.

Several researchers have found that vegetarians are more energetic, hard working and capable of lifting greater weight. They are peace loving and of jovial nature. They can exercise better control on their hunger and can undertake fast for longer period. Studies carried out in Japan have revealed that vegetarians not only remain healthy and disease-immune but also have greater stamina, longer life span and sharper intellects.

Thus, it is wrong to presume that non-vegetarian diet provides more strength than the vegetarian one. "The Nutritive Value of Indian Foods", published by the National Institute of Nutrition, Hyderabad, gives a list of comparative nutritional value of various food items. Some of the major items from that list are given below to enable readers to choose food items according to their taste and inclination and have more nutritious vegetarian food than meat, fish and eggs.

Contents of Every 100 Grams

Item	Proteins	Carbo-hydrate	Fats	Fibre	Minerals	Calories
Wheat	12.1	69.4	1.7	1.9	2.7	341
Barley	11.5	69.6	1.3	3.9	1.2	336
Bajra	11.6	67.5	5.0	1.2	2.3	361
Maize	11.1	66.2	3.6	2.7	1.5	342
Grams	17.1	60.9	5.3	3.9	3.0	360
Rice	13.5	48.4	16.2	4.3	6.6	393
Soyabeans	43.2	20.9	19.5	3.7	4.6	432
Rajmah	22.9	60.6	1.3	4.8	3.2	346
Urad	24.0	59.6	1.4	0.9	3.2	347
Lobia	24.1	54.5	1.0	3.8	3.2	323
Moong	24.0	56.7	1.3	4.1	3.5	334
Masoor	25.1	59.0	0.7	0.7	2.1	343
Moth	23.6	56.5	1.1	4.5	3.5	330

Arhar	22.3	57.6	1.7	1.5	3.5	335
Gram Dal	20.8	60.9	5.6	3.9	2.7	360
Ground Nut	26.2	26.7	39.8	3.1	2.5	570
Almonds	20.8	10.5	58.9	1.7	2.9	655
Walnuts	15.6	11.0	64.5	2.6	1.8	687
Cashew	21.2	22.3	46.9	1.3	2.4	596
Pista	19.8	16.1	53.5	2.1	2.8	626
Chilgoza	13.9	29.0	49.3	1.0	2.8	615
Kishmish	1.8	74.6	0.3	1.1	2.0	308
Gingelly	18.3	25.0	43.3	2.9	5.2	563
Water Melon Seeds	34.1	4.5	52.6	0.8	3.7	628
Coconut	6.8	18.4	62.3	6.6	1.6	662
Dates	2.5	75.8	0.4	3.9	2.1	317
Munnaqqa	2.7	75.2	0.5	2.2	1.1	316
Amla	0.5	13.7	0.1	3.4	0.5	58
Banana	1.2	27.2	0.3	0.4	0.8	116
Apple	0.2	13.4	0.5	1.0	0.3	59
Cherry	1.1	13.8	0.5	0.4	0.8	64
Grapes	1.0	10.0	0.1	–	0.4	45
Guavas	0.9	11.2	0.3	5.2	0.7	51
Lichi	1.1	13.6	0.2	0.5	0.5	61
Bel Fruit	1.8	31.8	0.3	2.9	1.7	137
Mosambi	0.8	9.3	0.3	0.5	0.7	43
Limes	1.0	11.1	0.9	1.7	0.3	57
Orange	0.7	10.9	0.2	0.3	0.3	48
Mulberry	1.1	10.3	0.4	1.1	0.6	49
Phalsa	1.3	14.7	0.9	1.2	1.1	72
Aru	1.2	10.5	0.3	1.2	0.8	50
Papaya	0.6	7.2	0.1	0.8	0.5	32
Mango	0.6	16.9	0.4	0.7	0.4	74
Raspberry	1.0	11.7	0.6	1.0	0.9	56
Water Chestnut	13.4	68.9	0.8	–	3.1	330
Carrot leaves	5.1	13.1	0.5	1.9	2.8	77
Radish leaves	3.8	2.4	0.4	1.0	1.6	28
Bathua leaves	3.7	2.9	0.4	0.8	2.6	30
Methi leaves	4.4	6.0	0.9	1.1	1.5	49
Palak leaves	2.0	2.9	0.7	0.6	1.7	26
Mint	4.8	5.8	0.6	2.0	1.9	48
Cabbage	1.8	4.67	0.1	1.0	0.6	27
Tinda	1.4	3.4	0.2	1.0	0.5	21
Cauli flower	2.6	4.0	0.4	1.2	1.0	30
Ladies Fingers	1.9	6.4	0.2	1.2	0.7	35
Beans	7.4	29.8	1.0	1.9	1.6	158
Potatoes	1.6	22.6	0.1	0.4	0.6	97
Tomatoes	1.5	6.7	0.2	4.2	1.2	35
Buffalo Milk	4.3	5.0	6.5	–	0.8	117
Cows Milk	3.2	4.4	4.1	–	0.8	67

Curds	3.1	3.0	4.0	–	0.8	60
Yoghurt	18.3	1.2	20.8	–	2.6	265
Cheese	24.1	6.3	25.1	–	4.2	348
Milk Solids	22.3	25.7	1.6	–	4.3	206
Skimmed Milk Powder	38.0	51.0	0.1	–	6.8	357
Yeast	35.7	46.3	1.8	–	–	344
Butter	–	–	81.0	–	2.5	729
Ghee (Clarified Butter)	–	–	100.0	–	–	900
Cooking Oil	–	–	100.0	–	–	900
Sugarcane Juice	0.1	9.1	0.2	–	0.4	39
Sugar (Cane)	0.1	99.4	–	–	0.1	398
Honey	0.3	79.5	–	–	0.2	319
Pork	18.7	–	4.4	–	1.0	114
Goat meat	21.4	–	3.6	–	1.1	118
Beef meat	22.6	–	2.6	–	1.0	114
Mutton Muscle	18.5	–	13.3	–	1.3	194
Fish	8.9 to 76.1	0 to 13.9	0.2 to 19.4	–	0 to 27.5	59 to 413
Eggs	13.3	–	13.3	–	1.0	173

Hence we see that the vegetarian food is not lacking in proteins and health giving elements. The cause of ill health of the poor children in our country is not a protein-deficit diet but it is their ignorance or inability to procure sufficient and balanced diet.

*From the above table, it is clear that non-vegetarian foods do not contain fibrous content (outer shell of cereals and pulses) at all and it has been scientifically well established that fibres play an important and exclusive role in warding off a number of digestive disorders and other diseases. Vitamins also are very necessary for our health and their best sources are also the vegetarian foods only.

Vitamin A : It is found in green vegetables, carrots, tomatoes and leaves of radish.

Vitamin B : It is found in green leafy vegetables and cereals.

---

* Medical Basis of Vegetarian Nutrition, published by Kishore Charitable Trust, Delhi

Vitamin C : It is available in green vegetables and in citrus fruits like lemon, guava, amla, oranges and mosambi etc.

Vitamin D : It is available in both animal and vegetable sources but its chief and best source is sun light in which it is available in abundance.

Vitamin E : It is abundant in Ghee and butter etc.

Vitamin K : It is available in green vegetables.

Thus all the vitamins essential for good health are available in vegetarian food and in sun rays.

Dr. Anna Spoerry of the African Research Foundation, after detailed study came to the conclusion that the Masai tribals, who are excessive consumers of meat, show a reduced level of cholesterol when they consume more curd. According to this study, the bacteria in the curd act as growth inhibiting agents for cholesterol.

+ Looking at the advantages of vegetarianism, the crusade for vegetarianism is gaining momentum in the Western countries. Salad bars are becoming very popular in America, from where people can take plates full of salad or canned salads to their homes. Different varieties of salad are made by supplementing vegetable salads with germinated grams etc.

Here are some news items published in Sandhya Times; New Delhi:-

Sandhya Times, New Delhi, 13th February,1990 :- London based property dealer Sardar Paramjit Singh, who was a successful athelete even in his school days, skips 2000 times every day and is well known as the "Skipping Sikh". According to him, he gets this energy from Chapatis (loaves of wheat flour). He is completely vegetarian.

\+ Ahinsa Sandesh, June 89, P. Box No. 85, Ranchi.

In Britain, people associated with vegetarianism are now regarded as modern, advanced and forward looking. More than a million people in Britain are now totally vegetarian and their numbers are increasing at an astounding rate. In Britain alone, there are more than 1000 health-food shops where only vegetarian food items are available.

In America the number of totally vegetarians have exceeded 50 million.

At the age of 92, Sardar Sujan Singh Kohli, father of Capt. Mohan Singh Kohli, who unfurled Indian flag atop Mount Everest in 1965, reads newspapers without using spectacles. He travels in city buses without any inhibition. His teeths which had given way due to old age are being replaced by the new ones. Sardar Sujan Singh Kohli, resident of J-Block, Navin Shahdara, Delhi, attributes the secret of his healthy life to pure vegetarianism.

Sandhya Times, New Delhi, 19 Feb., 1990:- American scientists, after years, of research on food have discovered the effect of nutritive elements found in fruits, vegetables, milk and cereals and are now working in the direction of curing dreaded diseases like heart troubles, cancer etc. by such food only. Many doctors have suggested that grapes, papaya, mango, melon, tomatoes and dark green leafy vegetables help reducing chances of cancer in the colon and other parts of the digestive system. Eating flesh-foods is one major cause of cancer. Drinking milk is one way to avoid cancer of the intestines. Those American women who consume vegetarian and fibrous foods are comparatively free from breast and uterus cancer. Incidence of breast cancer is more common in those who indulge in excessive intake of fats and flesh foods. According to a study conducted in Howard, an undeniable link has been established between the consumption of animal foods and the cancer of uterus.

*Naik Yadunath Singh who won the Paramvir Chakra award for his bravery on Kashmir front in the year 1948, was a strict vegetarian. One day his English officer challaned him and asked how he would get the required strength to fight the enemy from vegetarian diet. Naik Yadunath Singh requested the officer to arrange his wrestling with two flesh-eater soldiers at a time and if he is defeated he would start taking flesh-food but if he wins his vegetarian food quota be doubled. Naik Yadunath Singh came the winner and his officer not only permitted him to have more vegetarian food but also said that he too would take vegetarian food in future.

There are several such instances to prove tilt towards vegetarian food.

---

* T.V. Programme 22nd July, 1990.

6 Vegetarian Food – Cheap and Best

It is often said that eggs are a cheap source of proteins and nutrition. But this is a false propaganda. According to the table highlighting the percentage of proteins in various substances, given on Page 11, cost of one gram of protein comes out as under :-

*Material	Cost of one gm. of protein	Material	Cost of one gm. of protein
Eggs	14 paise	Pulses	3 paise
Wheat	4 paise	Soya Beans	2 paise

Looking from energy point of view, the cost per 100 calories comes out as follows :-

Material	Cost of 100 Calories	Material	Cost of 100 Calories
Eggs	90 paise	Pulses	8 paise
Wheat	9 paise	Soya Beans	5 paise

It is thus obvious that as compared to eggs, pulses and cereals are a cheaper source of both proteins and calories, besides they provide other important nutriments such as vitamins, minerals, fibre, carbohydrates etc., which are almost non-existent in meat products.

The Government of India's Health Bulletin No. 23 makes it clear that the calorific value of vegetarian food is far more to that of non-vegetarian food.

**From the economical point of view, it has been concluded that to derive one kg. of meat protein, the animal

---

* Eggs - Pure Poison by Dr. Nemi Chand Jain.

** The Human Onchogene : Work done by Prof. R.A. Weinberg from Massachusettes Hospital and Others.

has to be fed 7 to 8 kgs. of vegetable protein. It has also been estimated that to obtain one animal flesh calorie, seven vegetarian plant food calories have to be spent. Data compiled by the American agriculture department shows that the land needed to graze an average animal can sustain five average families of human beings.

An average American consumes about 120 kgs. of meat every year and to obtain it about 1000 kgs. of food grains are fed to the animals. If the same Americans consume food grains directly then atleast eight people can be fed for a whole year with the same quantity as is required for flesh food for only one person. Professor George Borgstorm has estimated that the amount of plant food fed to the animals in America alone would be enough to feed half the human population of the world.

†According to Mr. Nitin Mehta of Surrey (U.K.), 90 percent of the land in Europe and America is used to raise fodder for their animals. As much as 90% of protein content of the animal's food goes to sustain their growth and only 10% remains in the form of its flesh. Out of this only 44% animal flesh is worth eating. Thus, for every 16 kilograms of food grains fed to the animal, one Kilogram of edible meat is obtained. The land required to produce the fodders to feed the animals to obtain flesh food is 14 times more than that required to feed vegetarian diet to man directly.

---

† Ahinsa Voice, July, 89.

7 *Utility of Animal World for Human Welfare*

Men and animals are dependent on each other and mutually complementary. If a man rears one animal then that animal in return, rears his entire family, besides serving him in many ways. The horse yoked to the carriage, the ox pulling the cart, are providing livelihood, to the whole families of those who yoke and drive them. Many people make their both end's meet by showing the feats of bears and monkeys and spend their whole lives depending on these animals.

There is a popular saying regarding the shepherds of Rajasthan that on the face of it shepherds rear the sheep, but in fact these sheep rear the families of these shepherds, because by the trading of milk, ghee and wool obtained from them, they make their bread and butter. †Some specialists have found sheep's milk useful in treatment of even hereditary lungs diseases.

*According to former Agriculture Minister, Shri Buta Singh's statement in Parliament "Two million animals are killed every year in licensed slaughter houses in India." This figure does not include the number of cattle butchered in unauthorised slaughter houses. The killing of two million cattle entails an annual loss of one crore tonnes of natural fertilizer which could have been obtained entirely free of cost.

According to Shri Buta Singh, the main cause of rising food-grain prices is the hike in cost of chemical fertilizers. "Fertilizer is the costliest input". If chemical fertilizers could be substituted by freely obtainable natural fertilizers from cattle waste, food-grain prices can be substantially reduced, and the

---

† Vir Arjun, 2nd July, 1990.

* Ahinsa Sandesh, July, 89.

huge subsidies which the nation provides for the fertilizers industry could also be saved. Besides this, the saving of scarce foreign exchange spent on import of fertilizers and the huge capital investment in fertilizer projects will also be diverted to other useful projects.

How many human beings does a cow feed? Let us make an estimate. If a cow yields an average of 10 Kgs. of milk per day for an average of 10 months in a year, it amounts to 3000 Kgs. of milk which can satisfy the hunger of 6000 persons once. In its 15 productive years on an average, a cow in its whole life can thus satisfy the hunger of 90000 persons at least once. But if the same cow is killed and its flesh used for eating, it cannot satisfy even one thousand persons one time. The same applies to goat also. Similarly, one ox serves to raise at least 40,000 Kgs. of food grains during its life-time, thus providing one-time satiation to about 60,000 people, apart from the services it renders in pulling carts, transporting freight and so on. The dung of these animals provides additional benefits by way of fuel, manure, gas etc. If all these benefits are taken into account, then it seems that by killing these animals we derive only that much benefit as if some one may derive from making tea by burning currency notes. Killing the goose that lays a golden egg daily is never a wise proposition.

Most of the people are aware of the part played by fish in cleaning water. According to a news-item published in Sandhya Times, New Delhi of 12th April, 1990 fishes are now being used in Bhopal to help eradicate malaria. For this purpose 25000 fish of Gambushia and Gappi species have been floated in ponds and other water reservoirs. These fishes destroy the mosquitoes in their preliminary, that is, larva stage and thus help in containing malaria and cleaning the environmental pollution.

According to news item published in Nav Bharat Times, of 11th May, 1990 a study conducted by Prof. Sarkar of Dacca

University revealed that owls offered better protection to crop by eating rats and numerous crop destroying insects.

Even frogs and snakes save our huge crops every year by eating crop destroying insects and rats respectively.

According to the Honorary Secretary of the Bombay Humanitarian League, Sh. Dashrathbhai Thakker, the animal world contributes Rs. 25,500 crores every year to our national wealth by way of milk, manure, gas energy and carrying our luggage by sweating out in the hot sun. Besides this, after their death their hides and bones are used in many useful ways. In fact, we must be grateful to these animals who give us so much material benefits and also serve us. If instead of being obliged, we send them to slaughter houses in return of their numerous services, then it is only an act of ungratefulness.

The indirect benefits flowing from any ban on the killing of animals are not less than the direct benefits mentioned above. Cheap manure will mean cheap food grains, fruits and vegetables, that will mean adequate food for the poor, leading to an enormous saving on the cost of treating the diseases now rampant because of malnutrition. Availability of food at low prices will bring down the cost index and there will be saving in dearness allowances etc. Labour agitations and strikes will be reduced, millions of man-hours lost due to illness and strikes will be obviated resulting in more productivity and low costs. National income will rise and we will not have to go abroad with a begging bowl for aid.

Thus, a ban on the killing of animals is not just a matter of religion, morality or compassion but also a prime pre-requisite for the economic uplift of the country and the health of the nation. This one step has the potential of solving all our problems and raising the level of life for every inhabitant of the country.

Those who wish to be happy and secure must learn how to make others happy and secure, otherwise nature has its own strange ways of punishment. Just as the destruction of forests has disturbed the environmental balance and compelled us to launch a compaign for protection of forests and plantation of more trees, we will have to launch a similar compaign one day to save animals and birds which are equally vital for the maintenance of our environmental and ecological balance of nature. Survival of animal world is a matter of our own survival. Delay will be disastrous.

Our own welfare depends upon following the maxim :

"मा हिंसात सर्व भूतानी" *(Ma Hinsat Serve Bhutani)* meaning do not inflict injury on any creature.

Let all be happy without any pain or misery.

8 *Flesh-Food – Inducer of Diseases*

Here are the conclusions reached by eminent physicians and scientists about the many fatal and intractable diseases which one invites by eating flesh foods :–

[1]Research conducted at the State University of New York, Buffaloe, brought to light the fact that more than 47000 children born in America every year suffer from various inherited diseases because of the consumption of flesh foods by their parents. These children can never grow up to be healthy adults.

[2]The 1985 Nobel Prize Winners, Dr. Michael S. Brown and Dr. Joseph L. Goldstein of America, proved that to prevent heart diseases it is very essential to stop the clogging of blood vessels from cholesterol. The presence of this substance in vegetarian food is negligible. It is maximum in eggs and in abundance in fatty contents of meat, eggs and animals in general. The consumption of meat and eggs, reduces the number of receptors in the body and increases the amount of cholesterol in the blood-stream. This makes flesh eaters vulnerable to heart diseases and problems related to kidneys and stones etc.

Dr. M. Rock of Britain disclosed after a survey campaign that vegetarians suffer comparatively less than non-vegetarians from infectious, contagious and fatal diseases. They are healthier, better built, calmer and intellectually superior in comparison with non-vegetarians.

---

1 Ahinsa Sandesh, June, 1989.
2. Kalyan, Gorakhpur page 571 and Hindustan Times, New Delhi, 1st Oct. 1986.

A weekly programme on vegetarianism on B.B.C. Television gave clear warning that meat-eaters face a serious risk of contracting fatal diseases.

[1]Fatal diseases like heart attacks, cancer, blood pressure, obesity, constipation, stones and diseases of kidney, liver, and contagious diseases are rampant in Western countries where meat eating is widely prevalent, while their incidence is less in India, Japan and Africa where most of the people are vegetarians.

[2]In a study conducted on the persons of Huja Tribe of age-group 90 to 110 years, it has been revealed that the main reason of their long life and sound health is their being vegetarian.

Two researchers from Gwalior, Dr. Jasraj Singh and Mr. C.K. Dawas, made a research study covering 400 convicts in the Gwalior jail. They found that out of 250 non-vegetarian prisoners, 85% were hot headed and of quarrelsome nature whereas out of remaining 150 vegetarian prisoners 90% were cool headed and of jovial nature.

American specialist Dr. William C. Roberts has stated that in America, the heart disease patients are much more among meat eaters as compared to vegetarians.

[2]American doctors also say that vegetarians have greater inherent resistance to diseases as compared to meat eaters. Non-vegetarians are generally prone to constipation which is an automatic breeder of illness.

[2]According to another report, there is an insect called the Brain Bug whose bite leads to insanity among animals although it takes about 10 years for full-blown madness to

---

1. Human Enchogene : Work done by Prof. R.A. Weinberg from Massachuttes Hospital, U.S.A. & others.
2. Ahinsa Sandesh, June, 1989.

develop. During this span of a decade, if any person eats the meat of such bug bitten animal, then that disease enters the body of that person also.

Eggs, animals, fish and birds also suffer from diseases like cancer and tumours etc. and it is well known that they are not properly investigated medically before they are slaughtered for food. Any disease not evident on their exterior goes unnoticed and its germs and viruses enter the body of the meat eater.

[1]In America alone more than 40,000 cases are reported every year in which people suffer from illnesses caused by eating disease infected eggs and meat.

[2]According to Health Education Council 90% of deaths due to food poisoning are caused by eating meat.

[3]Seeing its approaching death in the form of butcher in the slaughter house, the animal trembles with fear and shock. It stops taking food one or two days in advance. Fear and restlessness causes leakage of stools. When this excreta gets mixed up with blood, it becomes poisonous and harmful. Blood, semen, stools, urine etc. becomes part of the flesh. Before its death, the helpless animal tries hard to save itself and struggles for it. When struggle bears no fruit, its fear and anger increases, its eyes become red due to rage and froth oozes out of its mouth. This condition creates within the animal a substance called Adrenalin which increases its blood pressure and contaminates its blood. When man consumes this meat, this Adrenalin also enters his body driving him towards many fatal diseases. When chlorinated hydrocarbons are consumed along with Adrenalin, it creates a serious threat to heart attacks.

---

1. Ahinsa Sandesh, June 1989.
2. Food for a Future.
3. Hindustan Times, New Delhi 1-10-86.

Boric acid and other borates are used to preserve eggs and fish etc. These compounds accumulate in the cerebral tissues and cause a grave risk.

It is well known that bacteria multiply quickly in blood. Due to mixing of blood in flesh, infection of bacteria increases very rapidly. As soon as the animal dies, all life saving functions cease and bacterial infections proliferate inside the fastering carcase. The onset of contamination is very fast in flesh as compared to vegetarian food. Eating this meat is almost like canibalism, when this meat reaches within the body of man, it gives rise to such incurable ailments which do not leave the meat eaters till their death. One who eats meat today, gets ultimately eaten by that meat one day.

The degree of harmfulness, pollution, dirt and disease in meat obtained from a slaughter house can be estimated from the fact that even European slaughter-houses equipped with the most modern technical devices are not considered ideal by the health authorities, not to speak of the warm, humid and dusty conditions prevailing in India.

The following are findings of the latest researches on the nexus between meat-eating and diseases :–

[1]Prof. Egnerberg of Germany found that "eggs produce 51.83% of phlegm (cough) and disturb the balance of nutritive elements within the body".

[1]Dr. E.B. Emary of America and Dr. Inha of England have clearly admitted in their books "Latest knowledge on Nutrition and Nature of Patients" that eggs are poison for human beings.

[1]Dr. R.J. William of England came to the conclusion that "Initially egg-eaters may quite possibly feel more energetic but later they fall prey to dreaded diseases like heart trouble, eczema, paralysis etc.".

---

1. Anda Zahar hi Zahar.

[1]Experiments indicate that if eggs are left at more than 8°C for more than 12 hours, the process of decay starts within their shells. Under the circumstances, in a country like India, where the temperature is always more than this, and it takes about 24 hours for the eggs to reach from poultry farm to the sales counter, the process of contamination is already started as it is not possible to keep the eggs from their procurement to selling in refrigerators. During the process of decay, the watery component of the egg first begins to evaporate through the shell, then it is invaded by disease germs which penetrate the outer membrance of the egg and make it completely putrid. These minutely contaminated eggs are consumed due to their non-recognition resulting in stomach disorders, food-poisoning etc.

[2]According to Mr. Nitin Mehta of U.K., about 5 million persons are infected by Salmonella every year. The N.H.S. says that it spends more than 2 million dollars every year for the treatment of food poisoning caused by eggs and chicken.

Besides Salmonella, the incidence of Listeria is also on the increase which causes flue resulting in Meningitis and Food-poisoning. It can lead to the possibility of abortion in expectant mothers and disease to the foetus. According to the Health department, Listeria was found in 12 per cent of the Ready-to-eat poultry food samples. A brain disease called Creutzfeldt Jacob's disease is caused by consumption of beef. This is similar to a disease in sheep called scrapie. It has been known to pass into human beings from animals through the eating of meat.

[3]In Australia which leads in meat consumption, and where average yearly consumption of beef is 130 Kgs. per person, the occurrence of cancer of intestines is maximum. Dr. Andrew

---

1. Anda Zahar hi Zahar.
2. Ahinsa Voice, July 1989.
3. Role of Vegetarian Diet in Health and Disease.

Gold, in his book "Diabetes : Its causes and treatment" has advised to take vegetarian food only.

[1]Indicated below are some of the most intractable diseases which research has shown to be caused by meat eating :–

Heart Trouble and High Blood Pressure : – The main cause of these diseases is the deposition of cholesterol on the inner walls of the blood-vessels. Eggs are the main source of cholesterol, followed by meat and milk-fats. The consumption of 100 grams of eggs per day amounts to an intake of 2-1/2 times more than the needed cholesterol.

Epilepsy : – It is caused by eating infected meat and unwashed vegetables.

Ulcerative Colitis, Appendicitis, Cartinoma of Colon and rectum :–These diseases occur more among non-vegetarians than among vegetarians.

Kidney Diseases : – Protein-rich food can damage the kidneys. Vegetarian food, being bulky and palatable, satiates the appetite quicker, so that one can not eat too much protein through vegetarian food, while excess intake of proteins through non-vegetarian food is very likely.

[1]*Rheumatoid Arthiritis, Gout & other Types of Arthiritis :* – Flesh-foods increase the amount of uric acid in the blood. Deposits of this acid on the joints cause these diseases. It has been observed that discontinuation of meat, eggs, tea, coffee etc. brings relief to the patients suffering from these diseases.

Atherosclerosis :– It means swelling of Arteries which is caused by excess of polysturated fats, cholesterol and calories in our food. Flesh-foods and eggs are rich in these factors while vegetarian foods have very little of them. Their presence is almost negligible in fruits and vegetables. The result is that vegetarians avoid falling victims to atherosclerosis.

---

1. Medical Basis of Vegetarian Nutrition.

[1]*Cancer :–* This fatal disease is found far more among non-vegetarians than among vegetarians.

[2]*Intestinal decay :–* Eating meat and eggs leads to dysentry, indigestion etc. in a chronic form, the digestive system gets depilitated and the intestines begin to rot.

[2]*Destruction of Immune System :–* Consumption of meat and eggs destroys body's capability for fighting toxins in the blood stream. The body becomes unable to defend itself even from minor diseases. Mind and memory are weakened. Development is retarted. Some American and British doctors have described eggs as a poison for human beings.

[1]*Skin Diseases, Eczema, Pimples etc. :–* Vitamin A is very important for the safety of skin. It is abundantly found in carrots, tomatoes and green vegetables. These vegetarian foods protect the skin, while meat, eggs, alcohol etc. increase the occurance of skin diseases. Most of the patients suffering from burning sensation of the skin are found to be meat eaters.

[1]Other diseases, such as migraine, menses – related disorders and ailments among women, infections etc. are more common in non-vegetarians.

In short, we can say that vegetarian foods prevent all types of diseases whereas non-vegetarian foods increase the risk and help in growth of most diseases. Vegetarian foods promote longevity while non-vegetarian foods cut life short.

---

1. Medical Basis of Vegetarian Nutrition.
2. Anda Zahar Hi Zahar.

9 [1]No Eggs are "Vegetarian"

Eggs are of two kinds – those which can hatch out into young ones and those which can not. Hens can lay eggs in their younger days even without coming into physical contact with the cocks. These eggs are comparable only to menstrual flow among women. Just as women expel the menstrual matter every month, hens lay eggs periodically. These eggs are an explusion of unwanted matter from the hen's uterus. To make more money out of these eggs, commercial promoters are now describing them as vegetarian eggs, *ahinsak* eggs, and other misleading names but these are obviously not vegetable products. They emerge from within an animal's body. Vegetable foods are the product of the earth interacting with sun, water, air and other elements while no eggs are born of the earth. Both kinds of eggs are laid by the hen and the chemical composition is also the same. If at all a distinction has to be made, such eggs can be called immature, dead or still-born, but not vegetarian by any stretch of imagination. In any case, both types of eggs have same harmful effects.

Here is how the hens are atrociously treated to obtain such eggs in larger quantities for quick commercial gains. What cruel methods are used, how the hens are kept in horried conditions to make the poultry-farming business more lucrative? The tortuous ways in which the hens are made to lay eggs and this horror and torture encapsulated in the eggs enters the belly and then the blood stream of those who eat them.

The eggs laid by the hens are not laid in the natural course, nor by their own volition. Rather, they are given hormones and injections of egg-formulations which make them

---

1. Anda Zahar hi Zahar.

lay eggs continuously. As soon as the eggs emerge, they are put into an incubator so that chicks can hatch out within 18 days instead of natural 21 days.

As soon as the chicken emerges from the egg, the males and female chicks are separated. The females are fed a special type of diet to hasten their maturity, they are kept constantly awake through out day and night under artificial bright light. This is done to make them eat more and more so that they may start laying eggs soon. Now these are kept in small cages instead of the natural ground and earth. So many hens are crowded in the cages that they cannot even flutter their wings. In the tense crowd, they peck at each other, get wounded, become irritated and suffer tortures. As soon as these hens lay eggs, these eggs roll out of a grader net and the hens are deprived of the instinctive satisfaction of brooding over the eggs. This is done because a hen which does not sit on the egg lays another egg quickly. In this way these hens remain confined in these cages for their lives. Their limbs become immobile due to lack of exercise. In order to obtain more eggs than they would have laid in the normal manner, the hens are fed with special diet containing dry fish. When their eggs-laying capacity diminishes, these are sent to the slaughter houses.

How can eggs extracted in this manner be called vegetarian?

10 *Various Religions Ban Flesh-Foods*

Scriptures of all religions all over the world, have taught us to see a reflection of the Heavenly Father in every living being and have considered non-violence as the best religion. Most religions have detailed the harm done by eating meat and called it an enemy of the longevity and a cause of degradation. But all the religions have prohibited the killing of any harmless and innocent living being. Some people who consider the satisfaction of their appetites the prime objective of their lives try to show, in pursuance of their self-interest, that their religion does not prohibit meat-eating, but that is untrue.

Hinduism : All Hindu Scriptures unanimously consider every living being a part of God and lay the utmost stress on *ahinsa,* compassion, love, forgiveness and such other virtues. Meat eating has been described as totally abjurable, sinful and leading to the decline of the soul. In the, *"Anushasana Parva"* of the Mahabharat, Bhishma Pitamaha has described as the sinners all those who eat meat, those who trade in meat and those who kill animals for their flesh. He said that any one who desires to increase his own meat by consuming meat of others will never be able to live in peace wherever he might be born. Those who eat the flesh of other living beings will themselves be eaten by the latter in a subsequent reincarnation. Any living being that is slain proclaims:

"Mas Bhakshyate yasmad Bhakshishya Tampapyaham"

i.e. "Today, he consumes me, some day I will eat him"

The Srimada Bhagawat Gita lays down that there are three catagories of food:

Satvik Food such as fruits, vegetables, cereals, pulses, nuts, milk, butter etc. which promote longevity, intellect and strength while granting pleasure, peace of mind, compassion, non-violence and equanimity, and saving the body, heart and mind from all impurities.

Rajasik food includes very hot, sour, bitter, spicy and dry substances. This kind of food creates perverted feelings, sorrow, disease and tensions.

Tamsik food such as stale, juiceless, half-cooked, evil smelling, rotting, impure, intoxicating materials and meat, etc., which lead man to evil deeds, cloud their intellect, give rise to disease, laziness and other evil qualities.

According to the doctrine of rebirths set out in the scriptures, one attains to the human form only after undergoing eighty four lakh births in other forms. This leads us to believe that all living beings are related to us in any of the earlier births. Thus by consuming meat of a living being, we are consuming meat of any one of our relatives.

The Atharva Veda (8.6.23) prohibits meat-eating and foeticide in these words:

Ye Ammam Mas Madanti Paurusheyam che ye Kavi Gaurhan Khadanti Keshwastanto Nashyaamasi.

i.e., whoever eats raw or cooked flesh, and whoever destroys a foetus shall be destroyed by us from here.

In **Satyartha Prakash,** Maharishi Dayananda has said that meat eating makes a person's temperament violence prone. Those who eat meat and consume liquor, their bodies and semen also get contaminated.

***Islam**: All Sufi saints of Islam have laid great stress on leading a noble life, a life of renunciation and compassion, eating simple food and abjuring meat. They themselves

---

* Hansa Hira Moti Chugna.

avoided meat eating. Sheikh Ismail, Khwaja Moinuddin Chisti, Hazrat Nizammuddin Aulia, Bu Ali Qalandas, Shah Inayat, Mir Dad, Shah Abdul Karim etc., were Sufi Saints whose path was pious living, self-restraint, love and affection for all and vegetarian food. They said "Ta Bayabin Dar Bahishte Aden Ja, Shafkate Banumaye Ba Khalke Khuda" i.e. if you want to live in heaven for all times to come, then behave in a spirit of compassion and sympathy with the entire creation of God. The Iranian philosopher Al Ghazali has stated that besides pieces of bread whatever we eat is simply to satisfy our urges.

The famous saint, Mir Dad, said that anyone who eats the flesh of any living being shall have to repay it with his own flesh. He who breaks another living being's bone shall have his own bones smashed. Every drop shed of another's blood, will have to be accounted for by one's own. Because that is the eternal law.

The great Saint Sarmad condemned meat - eating by saying that the light of life is asleep in metals, dreaming in plants, awake in animals and completely alert in human beings. Kabir, addressing Muslims, makes it clear that even fasting (Roza) is in vain if its practitioner lets his tongue dictate the killing of living beings for the sake of its taste. Allah will not be pleased this way.

The Imam of London mosque, Al-Hafiz B.A. Masri, in his book "Islamic concern for Animals", has expressed sorrow about the excesses against animals in the name of religion. Quoting from the holy Quran Majeed and the teachings of the Holy Prophet Muhammad, he described all acts of torturing of animals, and even keeping birds in cages as sin. According to him even cutting of trees is prohibited in Islam. On page 18 of his book the Imam Saheb has repeated the saying of the Holy Prophet Muhammad as under :

"There is no one who kills (Even) a sparrow or anything

smaller, without its deserving it, but God will question him about it."

"He who takes pity (Even) on a sparrow and spares its life. Allah will be merciful on him on the day of Judgement."

The Imam Masri is himself a vegetarian and advises everyone to adopt vegetarianism.

***Christianity**: Lord Jesus Christ obtained spiritual awakening from John the Baptist, who was a strict opponent of meat eating. The two main principles of the teachings of Jesus Christ are: Thou shall not kill and Love thy neighbour. The views of Jesus Christ in his Gospel of Peace are, "The truth is that one who kills others, is, in fact, killing himself. Whosoever eats flesh of an animal after killing it, is actually eating his own flesh himself. The death of an animal is the death of him who kills the animal because the revenge or punishment for this crime cannot be less than death itself." Again: Kill not the harmless animal, nor eat the flesh of your innocent prey, lest you become a slave of Satan. He further said: Vegetarian food will give you life and strength but if you eat dead food (meat) your food will kill you because life begets life and death always begets death.

***Sikhism**: The Gurbani, for the followers of the Guru, lays the principle of "Anna Pani Thora Khaya" meaning eat and drink less than your needs. Guru Arjan Dev has compared true lovers of God to the Swans and have named others as cranes. He said that diet of Swans consists of pearls whereas cranes feed on fish and frogs,

"Hansa Hira Moti Chugna, Bagu dada Bhalan Jave"

Adi Granth Page 960

The "Prashad" served in Gurudwara is always vegetarian Guru Nanak Dev always consumed only vegetarian food.

---

* Hansa Hira Moti Chugna.

The Gurbani clearly prohibits violence and professes love and compassion for fellow living beings:

"Hinsa Tou Man Te Nahin Chuti Jia Daiya Nahin Pali"

Adi Granth Page 1253

Kabir Sahib's teachings of pity, non-violence and his condemnation of meat-eating have been highlighted at various pages in the Adi Granth. All Guru Sahibs have very clearly forbidden violence. And when violence is prohibited, the question of eating fish, fowl and flesh does not arise. After years of intensive research, the Shiromani Gurudwara Prabhandak Committee has published the orders and edicts of the Gurus in the form of a book. One of those Hukum-namas reads as follows.

Hukum-nama No. 113 Page 103
Hukum-nama Baba Banda Bahadurji
Mohar Farsi
Dego Tego fatehi nusrat bedring
yaft az Nanak Guru Gobind Singh
I Oh Fateh Darsanu

"It is the order of the True Lord to the entire body of the Khalsa . . . . that they shall abstain from bhang, tobacco, opium, alcohol and desist from eating meat, fish, onions, nor indulge in theft and lust."

The food in the Langar of all Sikh Gurudwaras is compulsorily vegetarian.

Jainism: Ahinsa is the most important principle of the Jain faith. The Jain scriptures list 108 forms of violence. Violence in thought and actions, indulging in violence one self or getting others to use violence or abetting violence by others, are all forbidden. Even to contemplate violence is a sin. Violence is manifested in thought, word and deed. Even the utterance of words which hurt another person is considered as a sin. In a religion where tying up of animals, causing hurt to them, overloading them or even keeping them in cages is considered sinful, the question of eating meat just does not arise.

***Buddhism**: According to Buddhism's Panchsheel (which means five principles of correct actions), the first and main principle is not to torture any living being i.e. non-violence. The fifth and final principle forbids the use of liquor and other intoxicating things. According to the 8th Kand of the Sutra of Lankavatara, in the long chain of births and rebirths every living being has at one time or other been related to every other living being. It directs every body to treat all living beings as their own kith and kin. Even in an emergency the intake of meat is not considered justified. Only that food is advised suitable which does not contain flesh or blood or does not have life producing elements.

Thus, we see that every religion admits the presence of God in every living being. They have taught non violence and compassion and prohibited the eating of meat.

---

* Hansa Hira Moti Chugna

11 All Great Persons Condemned Flesh-Food

Looking at the world's history we find that all great scholars, philosophers, scientists, artists, poets, writers and religious leaders of the world like Pythagoras, Plutarch, Newton, Leonardo da Vinci, Dr. Annie Besant, Albert Einstein, Rev. Dr. Walter Walsh, George Bernard Shaw, Tolstoy, the poets Milton, Pope, Shelley, the Greek philosophers Socrates and Aristotle were all purely vegetarian. The vegetarian diet enlightened their minds and blessed them with the noble qualities of tolerance, compassion, love and non-violence.

The great scientist, Albert Einstein believed that "Vegetarian food leaves a deep impression on our nature. If the whole world adopts vegetarianism, it can change the destiny of humankind." Leonardo-da-Vinci used to pay for caged birds and set them free. He said, that if man wants freedom then why to keep birds and animals in cages.

St. Mathew and St. Paul considered meat eating an indicator of religious degradation. Methodists and Seventh Day Adventists strictly forbid the eating of meat and the drinking of alcohol. Tolstoy and Dukhobor (Orthodox Russian Christian) were of the opinion that meat-eating is against the tenets of christianity.

Adoption of vegetarianism by Roman poet Saneka, a disciple of philosopher Pythagoras, gave a pleasant and wonderful experience to him. He found his mind more healthy, alert and capable.

In one of his poems George Bernard Shaw wrote as under and compared meat-eaters with walking graves.

We are living graves of murdered beasts
    slaughtered to satisfy our appetites
Like Carrion Crows we live and feed on meat
    regardless of the sufferings and the pain.

Doctors once advised Bernard Shaw, he would die if he did not take to meat; his reply was that death was preferable to eating meat. He said he hoped that if he survived his doctors would also turn vegetarians, he did survive without taking meat. That great man preferred death to eating flesh of his fellow living beings.

Similarly, when Mahatma Gandhi's son became seriously ill he was told by doctors that the boy would not remain alive without meat soup. Mahatma Gandhi refused to take their advice, regardless of consequences. The son survived without consuming meat soup.

Chanakya said that those who eat meat or drink alcohol are animals in human form and a burden on a suffering earth.

Ramana Maharishi called non violence the Supreme Dharma and directed the consumption of Satvika food such as fruits, milk, leaves, cereals etc. in a specific quantity.

All great Indian saints and seers like Kapila, Vyasa, Panini, Patanjali, Shankaracharya, Aryabhatta etc. and all Sufi saints of Islam and all the great apostles of peace like Mahatma Buddha, Bhagwan Mahavir, Guru Nanak and Mahatma Gandhi who taught the lesson of non-violence "*Ahinsa Parmodharma*", were all pure vegetarians and were against the eating of flesh-food, because right thinking and spiritual attainments are not possible with meat-eating.

The famous poet, Coleridge has summed up the essence of all religions in his poem "Rime of the Ancient Mariner".

He prayeth best who loveth best
All things great and small,
For the dear God who loveth us
He made and loveth all.

12 Meat-eating Cause of Moral and Spiritual Degradation

Human feelings determine human deeds. Any man who harbours feelings of ahinsa, compassion, benevolence, etc., in his heart will never do or incite others to do any act which may cause pain to other living beings. He who is moved at the sight of any living being in trouble, cannot even think of eating meat. But those who have contrary feelings, those who have a tendency to torture, kill and make others suffer for their own selfish ends, will not shrink from eating meat or indulging in any mean or immoral act. He whose feelings are not hurt by the knifing of an animal will not have any fear or hesitation in shooting even human beings. He who can have animals butchered for the sake of his taste-buds or for accession of energy to his body will not hesitate to commit or abet violence for the fulfilment of his ambitions in trade, status, prestige etc. Can a person whose selfishness is his main driving force, be expected to follow principles of right code of conduct in any sphere of life ?

Meat eating undermines the equilibrium and the endurance of the mind. It stimulates the urges, cruelty and violent nature is enhanced. When a child is induced to meat-eating right from his childhood, he naturally adopts selfish attitude including causing pain to others and killing other living beings for food and fun for his own interest. His attitude becomes generalised so that he feels nothing wrong in cruelty, torture, violence and murder in any context. Noble feelings of non-violence, pity, righteousness just do not have a chance to arise in his heart. Selfishness is all that grows in that soil which in turn does not stop him from acting against the interests of the community and the nation to secure his petty gains.

The main cause of growing wave of violence, hatred and evil deeds in the world today is the suppression of finer emotions and promotion of feelings of selfishness and cruelty, due to meat-eating.

Meat-eating fans and fuels the fires of urges and desire. The more these urges are satisfied, the more they increase. Their satisfaction is quite impossible. Any obstacles in the way of satisfaction of urges give rise to anger. Anger suppresses the sense of discrimination between right and wrong. It destroys the intellect, leading to misguided and mis directed deeds which end in total disaster. In other words, meat-eating leads us to our doom.

As has already been mentioned in this book a survey among prisoners revealed that 75% of them were meat eaters and only 25% were vegetarians. In other words, meat-eating promotes the tendency towards criminal behaviour also.

Thus, we see that besides other damages meat-eating is the cause of the growing violence, inhumanity and other evil deeds in the world. It is leading humankind to total ruin. It is the duty of each one of us to halt this trend. If we fail to do so, our future generations will have to suffer the gravest consequences.

It is often seen that persons commiting cruel and inhuman acts like murder and rape etc. do not indulge in these crimes in normal conditions. Before venturing upon their heinous deeds, they indulge in an orgy of drinking and meat-eating so as to dull the pricks of conscience, humanity and morality which might stop them from doing these misdeeds. Unfortunately, today, many people are eating meat only on false considerations of so-called fashion, modernity or social status. The level of morality of such people is abundantly clear and they themselves know it very well in their hearts.

Some vegetarians in order to show off their 'modernity' get their food prepared into the shape of birds and animals meat and consume it to look like non-vegetarians. Though such food is not harmful to their health, but it definitely affects their inner feeligns as action are the result of our feelings. While consuming such vegetarian food the feeling and satisfaction of eating flesh of slaughtered animals is definitely there. This feeling will drag us away from finer feelings of love, non-violence and righteousness. It will lead us to cruelty and violence and convert us one day or the other, to meat-eaters and will definitely convert our coming generations into non-vegetarians.

13 The Importance of a Good Vocation

Apart from the appropriateness of quality and contents of the food one eats, it is equally important to ensure that the money used to p chase the food is also honestly earned. The sages have said that the means adopted to gain an objective should be as good as the objective itself. It is only food purchased with money earned by honest means that breeds the noblest sentiments in heart and mind. No happiness can come from food bought with money earned by torturing others. Such food will not be beneficial, rather, it will prove to be harmful and tending to perpetration of misdeeds. Thus alongwith our food, our vocation should also be good. Money earned by righteous means stays with us, keeps us on the right track and brings happiness. Wealth gained by violence and fraud is transitory, tends to be misused and causes grief. Wealth tends to be squandered as rapdily as it is accumulated. Dacoits, smugglers and those engaged in professions involving violence throw away their money on intoxicating materials, wine and women. On eating food brought from such ill-gotten money, the progeny of these people also learn such misdeeds. If we venture to look at our surroundings, we shall find that the families earning money by evil means never prosper. Their family members are addicted to intoxicants, suffering from ailments and are always quarelling among themselves. They never enjoy peace of mind and contentment.

Even a prostitute earns a lot from her profession, but how many people would like to dine at her place. The ingredients used in her food would be much the same as in the food cooked in a religious place, but the latter is called "prasad" because it comes out of money donated with faith and devotion, not money extracted by greed and lust or other unjust motivations.

Thus alongwith 'Satvik' diet, our professional dealings should also be good and pure. Food procured with money earned by killing or abetting the killings of living beings, can never bestow health, happiness and peace of mind. Hence, money earned from following professions is not considered pious :—

(i) Killing or arranging to kill birds and animals for food.
(ii) Encouraging fighting between animals, cocks and bulls etc. for fun and recreation.
(iii) Fabrication of articles of leather, silk fats, oils and feathers in which any living being is killed.
(iv) Trapping birds and earning from their sales.
(v) Trading in liquor and other intoxicating materials or abetting such trade.

He who kills himself or causes animals to be killed for food is as much a sinner as the one who eats such food.

14 The "Auto-biography" of a Goat

Like all other animals, after traversing through many rebirths, when I entered into my mother goat's womb, and suffered the ignonimity of being encaged there for five months and took birth, I found this world a nice and pleasant place to live in. Man and his little children treated me with affection, held me in their laps and gave me tender green leaves to eat. Drinking my goat-mother's milk, I began to grow quickly. Her master used to pet me and take me to his farm, where I used to feed myself on green leaves. He was not annoyed even when I evacuated my body-waste in his field. When I asked my mother the reason for this, I was told that our waste turns into manure for his plants, giving him great yields. That is why he was never angry with me.

Time continued to pass gradually and I went on living contentedly with my companions. After about an year and a half, a stranger came to my master. They talked for some time and then my master brought together about 40-50 of my companions and we were made to stand in a group. Then a big van arrived there and we were forcibily thrust into it. I wanted to go to my mother, but could not. When I moved towards her, an ugly-looking man hit me with a stick. Helplessly, we squeezed, ourselves in the van. My head began to reel due to over-crowding. My companions were also in bad shape. Fear was writ large on every body's face and the jerks caused by the moving vehicle was scratching our skins. The day went by and night fell and another day and night passed but the van was constantly on the move. Twice the van-owners threw us some food but it barely sufficed to fill half our bellies. Next day, the van stopped in a big city. A tall, bearded man approached the van, he gave the van-owner something and we were all turned over to him. Our new master drove us with sticks to a house. He made all of us stand in the sun. Restlessness caused by sunshine, hunger and thirst, and to top it the fear of the stick were driving us towards our death.

After a long wait we were pushed into the house. A man sitting there was examining my companions with some tube attached to his ears. When our turn came our owner gave him some thing, and he sent us inside without checking. I could not understand this but a senior companion of mine told me that he was a doctor and it meant our death was approaching us. Already half-dead with hunger, thirst and tiredness, I lost all my appetite on hearing this and could not swallow whatever little was given to us. Even water hurt instead of soothing my throat. Then the door of an adjoining room was opened and what I saw there made me tremble with terror. My legs refused to carry my weight and darkness appeared before my eyes. Cries and wails of my companions coming out of that room made me weep. I tried to cry but the voice could not come out of my mouth and throat. I tried to run out but a man caught hold of both my hind legs and threw me into that room where a horrible person looking like a giant was slitting the throat of one of my companions with a massive knife. Suddenly, a thought flashed in my mind. Is this the same man who claims to be the descendent of sages and saints and who always sings the songs of pity and non-violence? No, this cannot be the same man because even wild animals, who are solely dependent on flesh diet, never indulge in such mass killing as he was doing. While such thoughts were passing through my mind, a man caught hold of my ears and pushed me towards that horrible man. The pain now turned my fear into rage, I tried to pull myself away, but in vain. My frustration resulted in boiling of my blood, froth started oozing from my mouth and involuntarily I passed urine and solid waste. But no one took pity on my helpless condition. Rather, two other persons caught hold of me. One caught me by the legs and the other one started cutting my throat with a dagger. Fountain of blood spurted from my neck and my entire body was filled with pain. Now there was no alternative, but to pray for instant death. I only wished they would kill me with one blow and not prolong my agony. But no, I was destined to suffer more because the knife went only half way through my neck. Death was still far away and every moment of this torture dragged on like an year. Cursing my fate and remembering God, I continued praying and waiting for death.

Darkness gradually began to descend before my eyes and I started losing consciousness. Perhaps breathing had also stopped. It seemed as if I am dead and messengers of death were carrying me to the sky. But wait-what is that? My body still lay in that slaughter-house and now two persons were pulling my hide away from the flesh and fat below the hide. They threw my hide on one side and flesh on the other. After some time, a person purchased my flesh and took it to the kitchen of a hotel. There a person sliced my whole flesh into small pieces. Probably, all these tortures were too little for this God like man, because it is his heriditary habit to rub-salt on the wounds and this was still due. Why they should leave it for me? So after changing my meat to pulp he not only added salt and chillies but fried me on fire too and thus gave ample evidence of his barbarity. I was wondering, what next, when I saw another person arranging my meat in a plate and taking it out of the kitchen into a big decorated room where a young couple was sitting. As soon as the plate was laid before the couple, the male among them started eating my meat with a flourish of delight. But the female sitting opposite him appeared to dislike eating my meat and it seemed that she was just giving company to her husband.

By now, I had reached the court of *'Dharamraj'* and was standing in the queue of many souls. The loud voice of *'Chitragupta'*, who was narrating the account of good and bad deeds of everybody, attracted my attention. On my turn, Chitraguptaji revealed that in my previous birth I had feasted on the flesh of a goat. As a consequence of that, I had to born as goat and offer my meat for others. He also revealed that the persons, I had seen in the hotel eating my flesh were my own loving children of my previous birth, whom I had loved so much that for their sake I had staked everything in life. "Now that they are eating your meat in their present birth, they will have to suffer similar punishment for this in their next birth" Hearing this my soul trembled. How could I like my progeny to suffer the same tortures as had been inflicted on me? I, therefore, requested Dharamraj ji to forgive all of them because I too, had forgiven them and wanted no revenge of any kind. Dharamraj ji took pity on me and graciously ordered that, since as a goat I had eaten only leaves and creepers, and had done no one any harm, and had forgiven everyone, I should be reborn next as a man. My soul was thus sent to earth to take the human life.

Entering into my next re-incarnation, I vowed that now I would behave with the utmost rectitude and be a votary of truth and non-violence. Far from killing any bird or animal or eating its flesh, I would desist from causing the least pain to any living being, nor do anyone any harm. I would always offer protection to every living being. With these thoughts, I entered the womb of my new mother.

15 Reply to Arguments of Non-Vegetarians

Given below are the answers to the arguments put forward, by non-vegetarians to justify meat-eating.

Question : Nature enjoins a struggle for survival. One living being preys upon another to feed upon it. So what is wrong about man feeding upon animals?

Answer : The struggle for survival is indeed a fact of nature but this does not mean to kill and eat others. Rather it means to fight for the defence of our own life and that of others. No doubt, some wild animals and animals of lower-orders live on the flesh of others, but animals of higher orders, such as the cow, horse and elephant etc. live only on grass or other plants. Many animals having shape and size similar to that of man like Apes and Chimpanzes survive only on fruits. Many animals help and defend the weaker individuals of their species. Then why not compare man with the nobler animals, like cow, ox, horse and elephant etc. rather than with the barbaric animals? One wrong cannot justify another wrong.

According to Bio-chemistry, the body structure of man is different from meat eating animals which goes on to prove that nature has not evolved the body of man as flesh eaters. Nature has also bestowed man with many materials and has given him the ability to produce food through the noble vocation of agriculture. It is definitely going to be condemned if the master of so many abilities and owner of a rich culture leads a barbaric life and acts against the whims of nature.

Question : If man is a vegetarian, why he has dog like sharp teeth in his mouth?

Answer : The so called sharp teeth in man's mouth are not like the teeth of dog but are like the teeth of apes and monkeys who are all vegetarians. Meat-eating has no relevance to these teeth.

Question : If animals are not eaten, will they not over-crowd the earth?

Answer : It is a false notion. The number of animals always remains within a reasonable limit due to hunger, diseases and other natural factors. Wild animals generally confine themselves to forests. Their balance of population is maintained by what is called the food chain. Man himself causes an artificial population boom among the animals he wants to eat. If men were to cease rearing such animals, their numbers would remain at a reasonable level.

Question : Will only my renouncing of flesh-food will stop violence to animals?

Answer : No, not totally but it will definitely decrease violence to animals to some extent. A further step will definitely be tread in the direction of achieving the goal. In the beginning only one person takes the initiative for every cause, others follow him. Your example will encourage others who come in your contact. Then with those examples many others coming in their contact will renounce flesh food, and so on it will go on multiplying. Thus only your renouncing of flesh-food means renouncing by several other persons too in the long run.

Question : If there is nothing wrong in killing snakes, lions, wolves etc. why is it bad to eat meat?

Answer : 'Live and let live' is the best dictum to follow. To defend oneself against an attack is justifiable. In self-defence, even the killing of a man is considered just, because the motivation is preservation of life, (self defence) not destruction of life. But to kill any animal for fun or for satisfaction of your taste buds is a sin and it is prohibited in every religion. In law also, killing anyone deliberately is considered a crime, if however a person is killed in self-defence, the crime is mitigated.

Question : Even when man treads the earth, many ants and insects are trodden under foot. So, what is different if other animals are killed?

Answer : A man's character is judged by his intentions and deliberate actions. If a man deliberately and knowingly crushes under his feet any harmless animal, then it is violence. But if involuntarily or in unaovoidable circumstances, some insects are killed, then it is an exceptional situation. But to kill others without any specific reason or to abet killing for food is plain murder.

Question : Botanical science tells us that plants also-have life. Then where lies the difference between vegetarian and non-vegetarian food?

Answer : There are two kinds of life on earth, animate and inanimate. Men, beasts, birds, fish etc. are animate life while trees and other plants are inanimate life. Fruits ripen on the trees and then fall of by themselves, branches and leaves may be lopped off a tree and new one arise in their place. Many plants are propagated by their cuttings. Others can be transplanted. But all this is not possible with birds and animals. No limb of an animal can grow by itself after cutting. Man cannot produce animals like plants from earth.

All the living beings are made up of five elements - the earth, water, fire, air and sky. All these five are present in man clearly and predominently. Only four elements - earth, water, fire and air are predominent in animals, while in birds only three air, water and fire are predominent. Two elements - earth and fire - make up the insects and only one water is predominent in fruits, leaves and vegetables etc. The rest four elements are in sleeping state in vegetables and plants. Therefore, eating vegetable foods consumes the minimum of factors. Saints and Sages do not pluck fruits from the trees, but they eat only those fruits which have fallen by themselves on ripening. Minimum damage to life is the basic criterion. There is no harm in obtaining fruits from trees but harm lies in their cutting.

It is better to carry ten kilograms load of sin by eating vegetarian food instead of carrying thousands of tonnes of load of sin by meat eating.

Question : Does not meat give more strength?

Answer : Pulses, soyabean, dryfruits and nuts etc. contain more protein than do eggs or meat. Much more than our body's requirement of protein can easily be had from vegetarian food. Besides, vegetarian food contains the vitamins, minerals, etc. which are very essential for health and development of the body. These items are completely missing in non vegetarian food.

Meat-eating gives the body not strength but a kind of unhealthy stimulation. The body receives an excess of nitrogen which creates uric acid and other harmful compounds in the blood stream. Just to expel these compounds from the body, a lot of energy is needed which the body's defence mechanism pumps up in a hurry to meet the emergency. This is mistaken as an input of energy, although in fact it is a depletion of the body's reservoirs of energy.

Question : Are not the meat-eating races of Europe, more civilised, learned and powerful?

Answer : Their civilization, power or learning is not a gift of non-vegetarian food. Rather, it is a resultant of their other qualities, such as discipline, application, co-operative working and extracting power from the forces of nature. As regards meat, many jungle tribes also eat meat but they are backward because they lack the other qualities. Europe itself is witnessing an energetic movement against meat-eating and in favour of vegetarianism. Hence, it is wrong to ascribe the power of European races to the practice of eating meat.

Question : What should one do if a doctor prescribes flesh-foods?

Answer : Nature has created so many vegetarian substances which can easily compensate the benefits of meat-eating and can serve the same purpose much better. Only protein and fats are abundant in non-vegetarian food and these can be obtained from pulses, nuts, milk and butter etc. So it is not essential to obtain them from meat only. In this context, the incidents relating to Mahatma Gandhi's son and to George Bernard Shaw are clear examples of doctors insisting that life would not be saved without non-vegetarian food but these people refused to consume meat and yet survived. Hence it is neither proper nor necessary to follow the advice of meat-eating by the doctors. It is better to select appropriate vegetarian foods in its place.

16 Why Kill Animals for Fashion and Beauty Aids?

Man resorts to killing of animals not only for his health and satisfaction of taste buds but knowingly or unknowingly he also consumes some such fashion items and beauty aids, soaps, shampoos etc. the making and testing of which involves killing or torturing of animals. Just as while wearing Fur cap he is not aware, that it is made of the skin of that Kerakul lamb who has been brought out of her mother's womb forcibly, he is also not aware of the suffering of animals while using some cosmetics.

*"Beauty without cruelty" an organisation based in Poona, after great efforts, has prepared a detailed list of beauty aids and cosmetics made purely out of vegetable products, and in the formulation or experimentation of which no animals are made to undergo suffering in any way. Some parts of that list are reproduced here for the information of our readers. Those who do not want to encourage killing of animals will definitely benefit from this list.

The name of the product is given alongwith the brand name in bracket. From the number marked before the product, one can see the name of manufacturer at the corresponding number given in the list of manufacturers.

ITEM AND THEIR BRAND NAMES

CREAMS, LOTIONS & OILS

[1]Beauty Oil **(OLIO CAMPBELL)**, [2]Beauty Oil **(SHALAKS E. OIL)**, [3]Beauty Cream **(SUNDAR)**, [1]Baby Oil **(OLIO CAMPBELL)**, [4]Herbal

* Source : List of Honour, Sep. 1989, issued by Beauty Without Cruelty. 4 Prince of Wales, Drive, Wanowrie, Poona - 411 040.

Massage Cream **(CROWN),** [5]Skin Oil **(ELEGANCE),** [6]Sandalwood Oil, [7]Synthetic Essential Oils, [8]Calamine **(LAKME),** [2]Baby Massage OiL **(OLEMESSA),** [9]Face Cream, Lakshadi Massage Oil, [10]Astringent **(SUN),** Camphor Lotion, Facial Bleach.

[83]Snow **(NIKHAR),** [28]Snow **(VITAL HEALTH),** [32]Snow **(ATICK),** [83]Snow Vaseline **(HEMA),** [49]Face Cream **(COSMOLENE SNOW),** [85]Face Cream **(DOMA'S MYCO),** [86]Creams **(TIARA),** [87]Cream **(LAXMI),** [87]Cream **(VISHAL),** [4]Herbal Pimple Cream **(CROWN),** [50]Skin Cream **(NIVEA),** [8]Cold Cream **(LAKME),** [14]Foot Cream **(VRANA LEPAN),** [36]Vanishing **(MORNING STAR),** [8]Vanishing **(LAKME),** [67]Turmeric Vanishing Cream **(VICCO),** [76]Deep Cleansing Milk **(ANNE FRENCH),** [8]Cleansing Milk **(LAKME),** [50]Lotion Skin **(NIVEA),** [88]Beauty Face Lotion **(KESHAR GULAB),** [8]Hand & Body Lotion **(LAKME),** [87]Calamine **(ROSA CALAMINE),** [87]Calamine with Diphenhydramine **(CHANDAN),** [87]Hydrochoride Lotion **(CALASKIN),** [87]Tumeric Lotion **(BELA),** [8]Skin Tonic (LAKME), [8]Special Astringent **(LAKME),** [84]Vaseline **(HEMA).**

EYE-MAKE-UP

[11]Kajal **(SONIA, SRIMATI),** [12]Medicated Ayurvedic Kajal **(JAI),** [8]Eye Pencils **(LAKME),** [13]Kala Surma Powder **(ROBHICO),** [14]Surma **(NETRA JYOTI).**

[41]Kajal **(SANJOG),** [8]1Kajal Deluxe **(SHINGAR),** [8]Eye Liner **(LAKME),** [8]Mascara **(LAKME),** [8]Cake Eye Shadows **(LAKME).**

HAIR PREPARATIONS

Perfumed Coconut, Hair Oil, [15]Jasmine, **(MISTY),** Rose [5]Medicated Hair Oils **(SUJATA, BRAHMI, MAHABHRINGARAJ, SHEPHAL),** [16]Perfumed Hair Oil **(KING KOKO),** [17]Perfumed Hair Oil **(PAMPA),** [18]Hair Oils Natural Black & Dark Brown permanent Hair Dye **(GODREJ),** [19]Ayurvedic Hair Oil **(PETALCA),** [7]Hair Oil, [2]0Hair Oil **(COGONI),** [2]1Hair Oil **(FANTASIYA),** [1]1Hair Oil **(SONIA), 22**Hair Oil **(KESHUT),** [23]Almond Hair Oil **(LURE),** [24]Henna Hair Oil **(PALBRO),** [13]Hair Oil **(HIMKANTI),** [25]Hair Oil **(SAMRAT),** Hair Oils : Amla Tel, Brahmi Tel, [26]Brahmi Amla Tel **(BAIDYANATH),** Maha Bhringaraj Kesh Tel, Himani Kalyan Tel, Dandruff Hair Oil, [9]Kesari Hair Oil, Hair Oils : [3]Mahabhringaraj, Arnica **(CHITTI),** [14]Medicated Hair Oil **(BRAHMI AMLA),** [27]Hair Oil (RITA), [28]Hair Oils **(VITAL HEALTH),** Hair Oils : Amla, [29]Brahmi **(ZANDU),** Kuntal, [20]Hair Tonic **(COGONI),** [30]Hair Tonic **(TARJUNA),** [3]1Hair Tonic **(RICH FEEL),** [4]Herbal Hair Tonic **(CROWN),** [32]Brilliantine **(ATICK),** [11]Brilliantine **(SONIA),** [25]Brilliantine **(SHALIMAR),** [20]Brilliantine **(COGONI),** [17]Brilliantine **(PAMPA),** [33]Coconut Oil **(AO),**

[4]Herbal Hair Care **(CROWN)**, [34]Hair Dyes **(KEMP)**, [35]Hair Dyes **(FARISHTA, PEACOCK, SCISSORS)**, [18]Natural Black & Dark Brown Permanent Hair Dye (GODREJ), [36]Black Powder Hair Dye **(MORNING STAR)**, [37]Powder Hair Dye **(MOON & STAR)**, [4]Herbal Hair Cream **(CROWN)**, [16]Hair Fixative **(INNESCORT)**, [38]Hair vitalizer and Conditioners **(HERBALA DIE, HERBS & HENNA, HERBAL BEAUTY WONDERS)**, [39]Hair Lotion **(ARNICARE)**, [24]Henna Powder **(PALBRO)**, [40]Hair Tonic Powder **(SUKESHI)**, [40]Anti-Dandruff Oil **(DANDIKA)**, [9]Dandruff Hair Oil **(SHALIMAR)**, [25]Pomades, [10]Dandruff Lotion **(SUN)**, Hair Grower.

[84]Hair Oil **(HEMA)**, [85]Hair Oil **(DOMA'S MYCO)**, [18]Hair Cream **(GODREJ)**, [76]Hair Remover **(ANNE FRENCH CREAM)**, [83]Pomade **(NIKHAR)**.

NAIL POLISH & REMOVER

[41]Nail Polish **(TINA)**, [42]Nail Polish Remover **(NAIL MAGIC)**, [8]Nail Enamel **(LAKME)**, Nail Enamel Remover, [43]Plain & Frosted Nail Polish **(COSMACO)**, [44]Nail Lustre **(TIPS & TOES)**.

PERFUMES, COLOGNES & TOILET WATERS

[45]Handkerchief Perfume **(LINGER)**, [7]Perfumery Compounds, [21]Attars **(FANTASIYA)**, [17]Attars **(PAMPA)**, [13]Attars **(RABHIRAJ)**, [25]Attars **(SHALIMAR)**, [21]Perfumes **(FANTASIYA)**, [22]Perfumes **(SEAGULL)**, [17]Perfumes **(PAMPA)**, [46]Perfumes **(TOUJOUR)**, [25]Perfumes **(SHALIMAR)**, [22]Perfumes (Spray), **(MADAM)**, [47]Perfumes (Spray), **(SILPI'S)**, [21]Scent **(FANTASIYA)**, [13]Liquid Scent **(OTTO LALIT BAHAR)**, [46]Cologne **(TOUJOUR)**, [25]Ottos **(SHALIMAR)**, [28]Non-alocoholic Kerchief Perfumes **(VITAL HEALTH)**.

POWDERS

[48]Talcum Powders **(DELUX, ROLUX, BILUX)**, Talcum Powders : Lavender, [15]Rose, Khus, Jasmine **(MISTY)**, [49]Talcum Powder **(MOON DUST)**, [50]Talcum Powder **(NIVEA)**, [8]Talcum Powder **(LAKME)**, [25]Talcum Powder **(SAMRAT)**, [10]Talcum Powder **(SUN)**, [3]Talcum Powder **(CHITTI)**, [36]Talcum Powder **(MORNING STAR BEAUTY AID)**, [29]Talcum Powder **(SANTALC)**, [51]Face Powder Compact **(VRINDA)**, [25]Face Powder **(SHALIMAR)**, [52]Face Powder **(BHAGIRATHI)**, [22]Powder **(ABESH NIRJAS)**, [51]Khaki Face Powder **(BHARAT)**, [53]Medicated Powder **(NYCIL)**.

[83]Powder **(NIKHAR)**, [84]Powder **(HEMA)**, [85]Powder **(DOMA'S MYCO)**, [18]Toilet Powder **(CINTHOL FRESCA)**, 86Talcum Powder **(TIARA)**,

[8]Face Powder **(LAKME)**, [94]Face Powder **(MEIKO)**, [8]Face Powder Compact **(LAKME)**.

SOAPS & SHAMPOOS

[54]Shampoo **(SATIN DOLL)**, Shampoos : Lemon, [15]Herbal, Beauty **(MISTY)**, Shampoos : Special, [45]Luxury, Shampoos : **(LINGER)**, Beauty, [23]Shikakai **(LURE)**, Lime, [24]Shampoo **(PALBRO HENNA GLOW LITE)**, [55]Shampoo **(ARNICA)**, [39]Shampoo **(ARNICARE)**, [56]Alvareetha Shampoo Powder **(SILKESHA)**, Ayurvedic Shampoo, Herbal Shampoo, [10]Lemon Shampoo, **(SUN)** Pedicure Shampoo, Toilet Soaps : Jasmine, [57]Wild Flower **(AHINSA)**, Nandan, [58]Sandal Toilet Soap **(SANAM, CEPE)**, Toilet Soaps **(NEEM, JANTA, CEPE** (Luxury), [59]Ayurvedic Toilet Soap **(CHANDRIKA)**, [60]Soaps **(GEM, SAPNA DREAM, SAPNA SHIKAKAI)**, [61]Soaps **(SHAMPUCHI)**, [62]Soaps **(ROSE, JASMINE, KHUS, AMBER, PATCHOULI, SANDAL, MUSK, RATRANI)**, [63]Neem Soap **(HARRIS LIMDA)**, [63]Soaps **(RITA ARITHA, HARRIS SULPHAR, HARRIS SHIKAKAI)**, [2]Soap **(CETRILAK)**, [64]Soap **(ARITHA)**, [65]Soap **(KUTIR)**, [56]Shikakai Powder **(SHAMLA)**, [56]Powder **(SILKESHA)**.

[95]Liquid Hand Wash **(GOOLSHAN)**, [96]Perfumed Liquid Soaps Lavender, Jasmine, Rose, **(TAS)**, [76]Shampoos **(GLEEM BODY & BOUNCE, GLEEM SHINE & SHEEN, ,97Shampoos : Wild Chery, Camomile, Orange Blossom, Rosemary, Aloe Vera, (NATURELLE)** [8]Beauty Shampoo **(LAKME)**, [98]Soaps **(MYSORE SANDAL, JASMINE, SANSAR)**, [99]Soap **(NEKO)**, [52]Soap **(BHAGIRATHI)**, [63]Soap **(HARRIS CARBOLIC)**, [100]Soap **(HAMAM)**, [18]Toilets **(CINTHOL, NEW CINTHOL, CROWNING GLORY, MARVEL, VIGIL)**.

TOOTH POWDERS & TOOTH PASTES

[54]Tooth Paste **(KRISTAL)**, [66]Tooth Paste **(MOTI)**, [67]Herbal Tooth Paste **(VICCO VAJRADANTI)**, [68]Tooth Powder **(PROMISE)**, [45]Tooth Powder **(LINGER)**, [69]Tooth Powder **(DR. DEAN'S)**, [70]Tooth Powder **(GEMINI)**, [71]Tooth Powder **(NAFA)**, [72]Tooth Powder **(NIHARIKA)**, [73]Tooth Powder **(PRIDE)**, [74]Tooth Powder **(RAJARAJESHWARI)**, [75]Tooth Powder **(VEENA)**, [14]Tooth Powder **(SIVANANDA)**, [76]Tooth Powder with Astringent **(FORHANS)**, [56]Ayurvedic Tooth Powder **(JAINSON)**, [35]Herbal Tooth Powder **(FARISHTA)**, [67]Herbal Tooth Powder **(VICCO VAJRADANTI)**, [26]Red, Black & White Tooth Powder (Manjan) **(BAIDYANATH)**, [77]Lal Dantmanjan **(AMAR)**, [29]Dantmanjan **(ZANDU)**, [29]Dhavaldant **(ZANDU)**.

[68]Tooth Paste (**PROMISE**), [101]Tooth Paste (**BABOOL**), [28]Tooth Powders (**VITAL HEALTH**), [102]Black Tooth Powder (**JANATA**), [41]Kum-Kum (**KAMAL**), [11]Kum-Kum (**SONIA JYOTI**), Kum-Kum, [94]Kum-Kum (Bindi) (**MEIKO**), [39]Oral Antiseptic, [8]Liquid Make Up (**LAKME**), [23]Cold Wax Hair Remover (**LURE**), [35]Hair Removers : Soap & Liquid (**VENUS**), Liquid (**GULSHAN**), Soap (**GOOD NIGHT**), [40]For Chapped feet (**GAIRIKADI**), Herbal Nourishing Mask (**CREMETEEL**), Nourishing Mask (**PUMALMOND**, [103]Hair Removing Soap (**RAJARANI**), [87]Glow Liquid Make Up (**VISHAL, BELLA, LAXMI**).

TOILET PREPARATIONS FOR MEN

[18]Shaving Round (**GODREJ**), [18]Shaving Stick (**GODREJ**), [34]After Shave Lotion (**CONSORT**), [8]After Shave Lotion (**LAKME**), [10]After Shave Lotion (**SUN**), [46]After Shave spray (**TOUJOUR**), [34]Eau de Cologne (**CONSORT**).

[86]Shaving Cream (**MONARCH**), [8]Shaving Cream (**LAKME**), Lather Shaving Creams (**GODREJ**): [18]Rich Foam, Menthol Mist.

LIPSTICKS

[8]Lispsticks (**LAKME**), [88]Lipsticks, [89]Lip Lustre (**TIPS & TOES**).

PERFUMERY PRODUCTS

[91]Perfumed Paper Napkins (DEEPAK), Perfume Essences (**KIKU**), [92]Aerosol Perfumery Products (**KIKU**), [93]Perfume Compunds (**LANA**), [94]Scent Spray (**MEIKO**), [87]Sachet-Concentrated (**BELLA**), Cream Perfume.

MISCELLANEOUS

[66]Agarbatti (**ELEPHANTA**), [27]Agarbatti (**ALFA**), [28]Agarbatti (**VITAL HEALTH**), [68]Air Purifier (**ODONIL**), [78]Facial Tonic (**CHANTHIK**), [79]Ayurvedic Facial Mask (**KANTI**), [79]Ayurvedic Massage Oil (**SWASTHYA**), [11]Dry Powder Kum-Kum (**SONIA SRIMATI**), [80]Powder Kum-Kum (**SREEMA**), [81]Kum-Kum (**SHINGAR**), Kajal, Sindoor, [23]Beauty Mask (**LURE**), [35]Powder Hair Remover (**VENUS**), [100]lackead Remover (**SUN**), Face Charmer, Face Pac, Facial Bleach, Facial Mixture, Freshner, Oat Meal Scrub, Outer Eye Lotion, Pimple Go, Rose Water, Skin Softener, [40]For Blemished Skin (**JIRAKA**), Face Pack (**NEEMAL**), Face Pack (**HERBEAU CARE**), Anti-Pimple Powder (**PIMPLEX**), Herbal Body Massage, Oil Herbal Massage, Oil for Women, Anti Perspirant, [46]Air Freshner (**TOUJOUR**), [63]Dog Soap (**HARRIS NEEM**), [2]Dog Soap (**CETRILKA**), [63]Dog Dusting Powder (**HARRIS NEEM**), [82]Sticker Bindi (**SHILPA**).

MANUFACTURER

1 Campbell Manufacturing Industries, Bombay
2 Shalaks Chemicals, New Delhi
3 Sunder Homoeo Sadan, Calcutta
4 Crown Herbal Products, Madras
5 D.K. Sandu Brothers Chembur Pvt. Ltd., Bombay
6 Government Sandalwood Oil Factory, Mysore
7 J.B. Shah & Co., Ahmedabad
8 Lakme Ltd., Bombay
9 Sri Aurobindo Ashram (Ayurvedic Section), Pondicherry
10 Sun Products, Poona
11 Kothari Cosmetics, Vijayawada
12 Western India Chemical Co., Bombay
13 Raja Balkrishnalal Hiralal Co., Bombay
14 Sivananda Ayurvedic Pharmaceutical Works, Tehri Garhwal
15 Bombay Soap Factory, Bombay
16 Frugtneit & Co., Calcutta
17 Pampa Industries, Sholapur
18 Godrej Soaps Ltd., Bombay
19 H.N. Giri & Sons, Bombay
20 Chhatrisa & Co., Saurashtra
21 J.P. Parekh & Sons, Rajkot
22 Nirjas Perfume Products Pvt. Ltd., Calcutta
23 Nahira (Cosmetic) Enterprises Pvt. Ltd. Bombay
24 Palbro International, Vyara
25 Shalimar Agency (Perfumers), Nandurbar
26 Shree Baidyanath Ayurved Bhavan Ltd., Nagpur
27 Veto Company, Madras
28 Vital Health Products, Visakhapatnam
29 Zandu Pharmaceutical Works Ltd., Bombay
30 Command Perfumery Works, Aurangabad
31 Menaxi Pharmaceuticals, Bombay
32 Adarsh Pharmaceuticals, Junagadh
33 Ahmed Oomerbhoy, Bombay
34 Kemp-Pharm Division of the Morarjee Goculdas Spg. Wvg. Co. Ltd., Bombay
35 P.L.J. & Co., New Delhi
36 The Star Hair Dye Co., Delhi
37 Izuk Chemical Works, Delhi
38 Hansa Enterprises, Bangalore
39 Kosmeein Homoeopathic Pharmacy Pvt. Ltd., Bombay
40 Puma Herbal Cosmetics, Nagpur
41 Kamal Products, Bombay
42 Cheryl's Bombay

43 Cosmos Manufacturing Corporation, Calcutta
44 Shingar Cosmetics Pvt. Ltd., Valsa
45 Care Cosmetics, Calcutta
46 Renosold Company, Calcutta
47 Silpi Aerosols Industries, Bombay
48 Beechamores Pvt. Ltd., Bombay
49 Cosmodene Laboratories (India), Bombay
50 J.L. Morison (India), Ltd., Bombay
51 Bharat Cosmetics, Bombay
52 Shri Bhagirathi Seva Samiti, Meerut
53 Glaxo Laboratories (I) Ltd., Bombay
54 Alembic Chemical Works Co. Ltd., Baroda
55 Dr. Wellmans Homeopathic Laboratory Pvt. Ltd., Delhi
56 Jainson Products, Bombay
57 Beauty Without Cruelty
58 Naulakha Engg. Works, New Delhi
59 S.V. Products Irinjalakuda
60 Bombay Extractions Pvt. Ltd., Bombay
61 Galinus Pharmaceutical, Surat
62 Gulab Singh Johrimal, Delhi
63 Rita Enterprise, Bombay
64 Teli Soap & Chemical Factory, Ahmedabad
65 Yusuf Meherally Centre, Tara
66 Bajaranglal & Sons, Titilgarh
67 Vicco Laboratories, Bombay
68 Balsara Hygiene Products, Bombay
69 Deen Brothers, Bombay
70 Gemini Chemical Products, Machilipatnam
71 Nafa & Co., Madras
72 Niharika Products (India), Calcutta
73 Pride Industries, Bombay
74 Raja Enterprises, Kakinada
75 Ranga Industries, Guntakal
76 Geoffrey Manners & Co. Ltd., Bombay
77 Kailash Chemical Works, Kantabonji
78 Darshana Traditional Products, Madras
79 Dharmatma Ayurveda Resashala, Akalkot
80 Sreema Industries, Hyderabad
81 Paramount Kumkum Pvt. Ltd., Valsad
82 Tips & Toes Cosmetics (India) Ltd., Valsad
83 Abdul haq, Nagpur
84 Dharmyug Industries, Gondia
85 Vijaya Chemical & Toilet Works (Circars), Madras
86 J.K. Helene Curtis Ltd., Thana
87 Vishal Cosmetics, Bombay
88 Jain Ayurvedics, Coonoor
89 Indian Cosmetic Industries, Delhi
90 Creative Cosmetics, Valsad
91 Deepak & Co., Thana
92 Kiku Fragrances, Bombay

93 Lana Floressens, Bombay
94 Meiko Cosmetics, Amritsar
95 D.K.B. Products, Bombay
96 Tas Products Co., Bombay
97 Ranbaxy Laboratories, New Delhi
98 Karnataka Soaps & Detergent Ltd., Bangalore
99 Parke-Davis (India) Ltd., Bombay
100 Tata Oil Mills Co. Ltd., Bombay
101 Besta Cosmetics Ltd., Vapi
102 Bamankar Brother's Industries, Dulia
103 T.P. Lal & Co., Udhna

17 How to Get Rid of Flesh-Food?

If after learning from this book the pros and cons of vetetarian and non-vegetarian food and the diseases which flesh-food invites, some brothers and sisters wish to renounce flesh food but hesitate due to compulsions of family, society and of their taste-buds, should in our opinion try the following :

1. Convert your wish of renouncing flesh-food into a strong will by reading the book again and again, because "where there is a will there is a way".

2. Let your mind have no doubt that renouncing flesh-food is a noble act of social reform and family welfare. It is an act of uplift and moving towards modernity. A person who makes use of new research and discoveries, is only called modern. Have pride in being a vegetarian.

3. It should be clearly understood that renouncing flesh-food doesn't cause any weakness. Rather, it promotes health and saves from many dreaded diseases like cancer, etc.

4. Some flesh-food looking dishes prepared from vegetarian products may be taken initially to satisfy the taste-buds. Then gradually switch over to normal vegetarian dishes.

5. Display in your kitchen and dining room some slogan like "Flesh-Food Breeds Diseases". This will help remembering the harms of flesh-food by all family members.

6. Every time flesh-food comes before you, think of the

tortures on the animals and ponder if tnat may be of the meat of some near and dear of your earlier incarnation.

7. If inspite of above efforts you fail to renounce flesh-food immediately then act on a package programme of limited duration, say seven weeks. Have only vegetarian food for one day in the first week and for two days in the second week and so on increase a vegetarian food day every week and be a complete vegetarian after seven weeks.

Renouncing flesh-food causes no adverse effect; just a strong will is needed. Several persons who used to take flesh-food daily renounced it at one stretch. You too can do it. Make up your mind and get rid of this disasterous food just today.

Bibliography

1. Ahinsa Voice by Sh. Satish Kumar Jain, Sharman Sahitya Sansthan, 53, Rishab Vihar, Delhi-110 092
2. अहिंसा सन्देश by श्री रतनेश कुमार जैन, अहिंसा सन्देश कार्यालय, पो. बा. नं. 85, रांची, बिहार.
3. अंडा : जहर ही जहर एवं शाकाहार क्रान्ति by डा. नेमी चन्द जैन, हीरा भैया प्रकाशन, 65, पत्रकार कालेनी, कनाडिया मार्ग, इन्दौर (म.प्र.) 452001.
4. कल्याण Issued by गीता प्रेस, गोरखपुर.
5. हंसा हीरा मोती चुगना by श्री संतोख सिंह, श्री टी.आर. शंगारी, राधा स्वामी सत्संग, ब्यास, जि. अमृतसर.
6. जीवन में शाकाहार by श्री सन्त दर्शन सिंह जी महाराज, कृपाल आश्रम नं. 2 करनाल रोड, विजय नगर, देहली-9.
7. Role of Vegetarian by Dr. O.P. Kapoor, Bombay Hospital Institute of Medical Sciences, 12 Marine Lines, Bombay.
8. Medical Basis of Vegetarian Nutrition by Dr. D.C. Jain, Kishore Charitable Trust, Delhi. (SR. N.K. Jain, 1059 Bajar Pai Walan, Jama Masjid, Delhi.)
9. Nutritive Value of Indian Foods by C. Gopalan, National Institute of Nutrition, ICMR, Hyderabad-500 007.
10. List of Honour issued by Beauty without Cruelty, 4 Prince of Wales Drive, Wanowrie, Poone-411 040.
11. Why Vegetarianism by Dr. Dashrath Bhai Thaker, Bombay Humanitarian League Daya Mandir, 2nd Floor Mumbadevi Road, Bombay-400 003.
12. सत्यार्थ प्रकाश issued by आर्य समाज प्रतिनिधि सभा, देहली.
13. Jane Brody's Nutrition Book issued by W.W. Narton & Company, Inc. 500 Fifth Avenue, New York 10110.
14. Food for a Future issued by Shree Akhil Bhartiya Hinsa Nivaran Sangh, Hinsa Nivaran Bhawan, 32, Manish Society, Mirambica Road, Ahmedabad-380 013.
15. Indian Vegetarianism एवं भारतीय शाकाहार by Dr. Tara Chand Agarwal, Barjatya Family Charitable Trust, Haldia House, Johri Bazar, Jaipur-302 003.
16. अहिंसा के अछूते पहलु by जैन विश्व भारती, लाडनूं, राजस्थान.
17. The Indian Vegetarian Congress Quarterly, Why Kill for Food by G.L. Rudd & the Vegetarian Why by Sri Surendra M. Mehta, The Indian Vegetarian Congress, 1, Eldams Road, Madras-18.
18. Flesh Food An Un-natural & Harmful Diet issued by Dev Samaj Prakashan, No. 3345, Sector 21-D, Chandigarh.
19. Why Do We Advocate Vegetarianism issued by Dev Samaj, Sector 36 B, Chandigarh.
20. मांसाहार क्यों घृणित व हानिकारक है issued by देव समाज साहित्य विभाग, चंडीगढ़.
21. सात्विक और योगमुक्त जीवन issued by प्रजापिता ब्रह्मकुमारी ईश्वरीय विश्व विद्यालय, पाण्डव भवन, माउँट आबू.
22. पशु जगत और उसके सम्बन्ध में मनुष्य के कर्त्तव्य by देव समाज प्रधान कार्यालय, मोगा.
23. Islamic Concern for Animals by Al-Hafiz B.A. Masri, The Athene Trust, 3A, Charles Street Petersfield Hants GU 32 3EH. U.K.